IMPRINTS III

Discovering the Historic Face of English Quebec

Quebec City – The Outlying Communities of Quebec City
St. Maurice – Beauce – Lower St. Lawrence – Gaspé
Charlevoix – Magdalen Islands – Saguenay – North Shore
Lower North Shore

By

Ray & Diana Baillie

Cover photo: Lighthouse – Bonaventure. (see text on p 154)
Cover and back photos and some of Gaspé and the Lower North Shore
by Patrick Baillie
Front and back covers designed by Studio Melrose/Ted Sancton

Printed in Canada

Price-Patterson Ltd.
Canadian Publishers, Montreal, Quebec, Canada
E-mail: michaelprice@pricepatterson.com

ISBN 1-896881-43-2

DEDICATION

To the staunch rural and urban English-speaking peoples
of Eastern Quebec who continue the struggle to retain
their culture and their heritage.

ACKNOWLEDGEMENTS

The authors could not have completed this book without the help of the following people:
Louise Abbott (Lower North Shore); Alex Addie (Quebec City); Janet Ainslie (Shawinigan); Ken Annett (Gaspé); Ray Barakett (Magdalens); Dr. Jacques Bechard (Ste-Claire); Lyndon Bechervaise (New Carlisle); Jean and David Bell (Arvida, Kenogami); Hugh and Barbara Bignell (Lake Beauport); Dwight Bilodeau (Old Fort Bay); Dr. Henri Bilodeau (Shawinigan); Louisa Blair (National School, Quebec City); Ronnie Blair (Quebec City); Hector Blake (Seven Islands); David Blinco (Quebec City); Gilbert Bossé (Metis); Rita Bourgoin (Port-au-Persil); Alan Breakey (Breakeyville); Frank Cabot (Murray Bay); Dr. Charles Cahn (Beauport); Arthur Campbell (New Richmond); Byron Clark (Magdalens); Leonard Clark (Old Harry); Eddy Conway (Shannon); Isabel and Lorne Crowell (Entry Island); Frank Delaney (Grindstone); Leonard Dickson (Entry Island); Tom Donohue (Murray Bay); Bill Dousett (Three Rivers); Joan Dow (New Richmond); Bernice Duffy (Arvida); Peter Dunn (Ste-Pétronille); Lincoln Egan (Ste-Agathe-de-Lotbinière); Keith Eldridge (Seven Islands); Dr. Ron Fletcher (Charlevoix); Riva Flexer (Shawinigan); Jean Ford (Portneuf); Leslie Foreman (Kegaska); Don and Charlotte Gamble (St-Georges); Jean Harnois (Shawinigan); Joan Harrington (Metis); Malcolm Henderson (St. Malachy); Graham Hill (Pont Rouge); Edward Hogan (Ste-Agathe); Doug Hunt (Pabos); Tom Huston (general research); Dorothy and David Jomini (Grand'mere); Stephen Kohner (Baie Comeau); Harold Lavallee (Middle Bay); Shirley Leary (Barachois); George Le Grand (Paspebiac); Peter Le Gros (Paspebiac); Betty Le Maistre (Gaspé); Wilhelm Loken (La Tuque); Karen Macdonald (Quebec City); Margaret MacDougall (Kenogami); Margery Mackenzie (Cap-à-l'Aigle); Mrs. Syd Maloney (Corner of the Beach); Bob Martin (North Shore); Rev. Stuart and Mary Martin (Cap-à-l'Aigle); David McCall (province of Quebec); Danny McCormick (Anticosti); Stan McGee (Shelter Bay); Clive and Diana Meredith (Quebec City); Helen Meredith (province of Quebec); Richard Michaud (Cacouna); Margaret Miller (Frampton); Médéric O'Brien (Seven Islands); Marianna O'Gallagher (Quebec City); Odin Olsen (La Tuque); Alex Paterson (Charlevoix); Rev. Curtis Patterson (Gaspé); Cynthia Patterson (Gaspé town); William Pearce (Metis); Gordon Pozer (St-Georges); Harold Price (Tadoussac); Michael Price (Saguenay and Quebec City); Ivan Quinn (Entry Island); Alexander Reford (Metis); Molly Richard (Portneuf); Meb Reisner (Quebec City); Russell Robertson (La Tabatière); Brian Rock (Baie Comeau); Rex Scott (Breakeyville); Donald Simons (Simons store); Marion Smith (St. Malachy); Larry Thomson (Portneuf); Brian Treggett (Mount Hermon Cemetery); Chester Turnbull (Grindstone); Ethelyne Vautier (Shigawake); Ed Vining (Three Rivers); Richard Walling (Quebec City); Cornelius Walsh (Blanc Sablon); Jim Whyte (Shawinigan); Walter Willett (New Richmond); Chandler Williams (Grand'mere).

A special thanks to our manuscript readers, whose help is much appreciated:
Alan Breakey (Breakeyville); Byron Clark (Magdalen Islands); Keith Eldridge (North Shore); Dr. Ron Fletcher (Charlevoix); Charlotte Pozer Gamble (St-Georges-de-Beauce); Malcolm Henderson (St. Malachy); Betty Le Maistre (Gaspé); Margaret MacDougall and Bruce MacDougall (Saguenay); Clive Meredith (Quebec City); Helen Meredith (*Imprints III*); Marianna O'Gallagher (Quebec City and region); David Price (*Imprints III*); Michael Price (*Imprints III*); Larry Thomson (Portneuf); Chandler Williams (St. Maurice).

Introduction to the Imprints series

English Quebecers, *"the forgotten people"*, have been portrayed in most history books as politicians and captains of industry. They must be viewed as more than governors and industrialists. English and French alike benefit from learning about the wider role of the English in Quebec, particularly their economic, social and cultural contributions. Their presence here goes far beyond the banks, railways and industry. Most English were ordinary men and women struggling to survive as labourers, farmers, shop keepers, doctors and educators.

Photographs, showing the range and variety of landmarks, will, we hope, help the story to come alive. We chose not to use archival photos, except for occasional portraits, showing only what is there to be seen today, though, sadly, some of our landmarks have already disappeared. We define *English* as those whose language was English when they arrived. This includes Irish, most Scots, English, Welsh, some Jews, and Blacks from the United States and the British Caribbean.

Our search for landmarks to photograph and for information has taken us on a travel adventure throughout Quebec, meeting both English and French, and learning so much about our province. We have consulted professional histories and drawn material from libraries, newspapers, historical societies, the Internet, and oral history.

Our aim is to highlight the presence and culture of the English who helped to build communities in Quebec, particularly before The Great War of 1914-18. We have purposely limited the roles of large corporations, churches and cemeteries, which have already been well-documented in other books. This is not a history of the English in Quebec, but history informs its pages. We do not provide comprehensive local histories, nor is this an architectural study or a travel book, though some will find it a useful travel companion. Our subjects are chosen to illustrate the role of institutions and of people, rather than for their architectural beauty, though many are indeed beautiful.

The "mainland" English (those living off the island of Montreal) have been migrating away from rural Quebec for well over a hundred years. They built the instruments which encouraged this mobility: education and the railways which gave them access to English North America. Many of the communities and industries that they built have been carried on and developed successfully by the French, particularly after the Quiet Revolution.

We regret it if we have omitted communities with an English history, and that we have left out some landmarks. In fact, our material has proliferated to such an extent that we have divided the book into three volumes: the first one deals with the area west of the Richelieu River, including Montreal; the second covers the Eastern Townships; and Volume III examines the Quebec City area and the eastern part of the province.

Yes, there has been friction between French and English in Quebec, particularly in the areas of politics, religion, and the control of economic power. But, so much emphasis is placed on the conflict and differences between the two peoples, that we want to stress what has been positive, where the French and English have lived in harmony, inter-married, learned from each other, and co-operated to build many of Quebec's communities.

We hope that this book contributes to a still greater understanding between the two peoples who pioneered Quebec.

Glossary of terms:

English: unless otherwise specified, e.g. "...most Scots, English, Irish....", *English* refers to English-speakers.

Landmark: any building or other site which shows what the English built. All of our photographs depict landmarks.

Use of accents: All French words and names are accented appropriately for French usage, except for Montreal and Quebec in keeping with English usage in the historical era that we cover.

We use traditional English place names where appropriate.

Seigneury/seigniory: we use the former when referring to the French régime, and the latter for those which passed into English ownership.

Trucking: (from the French "troquer" – to trade), the practice of forcing employees to take payment in goods.

Grandfather clause: the provision in law whereby Quebec children who have a parent or grandparent who was educated in English in Quebec have the right to an English education.

Contents

Introduction to Imprints III

When we began this book project in 1996, we had a general idea of what we believed to have been the role and presence of the English-speaking peoples of Quebec. The reality far exceeded our expectations and the vast and varied nature of the role of the English in the building of Quebec's communities was a delightful process of discovery for us. In 2001, *Imprints,* which covered Montreal and the western part of the province, was published; in 2002, came *Imprints II* on the Eastern Townships; and, now, we present *Imprints III* which considers Quebec City and the eastern part of the province.

Imprints III differs slightly from the first two books. While volumes *I* and *II* consider landmarks built mostly before World War I, this one covers the mid-18th century to the mid-20th since many of the communities on the North Shore were developed later. This volume also covers a much wider geographic area than the others, traversing eleven different regions from the St. Maurice to Blanc Sablon, from the Beauce to the Magdalen Islands. The various communities in whose early development the English played a role are spread out with little or no connection other than that their language of origin was English.

Among the English-speakers who helped to build this part of the province of Quebec are: the English and Irish builders in Quebec City; the Irish farmers who broke new lands in the areas surrounding that city; the American entrepreneurs who built the towns and cities on the St. Maurice River; the German-American Pozers, who developed St-Georges in the upper Beauce; the Fords and the Bishops who built the paper mills on the Portneuf River; the affluent businessmen and professionals who erected the magnificent summer homes and gardens down the Lower St. Lawrence; the Scottish seigniors at Murray Bay, Rivière-du-Loup and Metis; the Loyalists and Jerseymen in Gaspé; the fisher-farmers of the Magdalen Islands; the industrial developers of the Saguenay River and the North Shore; and the fishermen along the Lower North Shore.

Our search for the stories of the English builders of Quebec has taken us on a host of delightful journeys over the last eight years. We have met and been immeasurably helped by many wonderful people, some of them, sadly, no longer with us. Our avenues of research included the local historical societies where we often made our start in a community; interviews with local people and with descendants living elsewhere; and visiting the sites.

What surprised us most was the breadth and diversity of the English contribution to this province. The English founded a significant number of the communities, where their presence was substantial in the 19th and early 20th centuries. Though their numbers have dwindled almost everywhere, their legacy remains. Emblematic of this are the English place names still in use, sometimes in communities now almost entirely French-speaking: Forestville, Clarke City, Frampton, New Richmond, Wakeham, Old Harry – to name but a few; streets such as chemin Bishop, côte Dinan, the delightful chemin St. James Church, and even chaussée des Écossais. Names which arrived here from Scotland, Ireland and England – names such as Hogan, Blackburn, Ryan, Warren, Fraser – sometimes belong to French-speakers. And, some Lavallées, Féquets, Bedards and Phaneufs are now English.

In the midst of their declining numbers throughout the province, there are still hopeful examples of English tenacity: the vibrant culture of the relatively small populace remaining in Quebec City; the stamina of the people in the fishing communities of the Lower North Shore; and the English throughout the province who have remained when others in their area have moved on. Whatever the future, and despite this decline, the impact made by English-speakers on this part of the province of Quebec will endure.

INDEX OF COMMUNITIES

Quebec City

Quebec, a fortified town since the time of Samuel de Champlain, was the centre of the French empire in America for one hundred and fifty years when the fur trade was the dominant enterprise. Today, it is once again a primarily French-speaking city, the capital of the province of Quebec. In the interim, the English-speaking peoples made their mark here.

After the Conquest, Quebec became a centre of British power: government, the military, commerce and industry. This port city, with its ship-building and its traffic in furs and timber, reached the height of its maritime power in the mid-19th century. It was the port of entry for hundreds of thousands of immigrants, many of whom chose to settle in Quebec. The 1860-61 census gave the population of the city as 51,109 – of whom about forty percent were English-speaking. Three-quarters of these were Irish. At this time, the mayors of Quebec City included men of Irish or Scottish descent. Today, there are an estimated 15,000 English-speakers in Quebec City and the surrounding area – about two percent of the population.

The British influence on the architecture of Quebec City has been considerable. Merchants and professionals asserted their cultural identity and their confidence in the supremacy of British traditions in their architectural choices, often failing to take the Quebec climate into consideration, e.g. that flat roofs accumulated snow. Buildings such as the Anglican Cathedral of the Holy Trinity, and the Jonathan Sewell house are examples of British-influenced architecture here.

English-speakers once had their own districts within the city. Now they are dispersed throughout areas such as Sillery and Ste-Foy. "There is no such thing as a Westmount or a West Island here for the English. We are integrated, not assimilated, and we (French and English) get along very well." (Rosemary Cannon, former President of the Literary and Historical Society of Quebec [affectionately known as the "Lit & Hist"]). The decline of the English in the city begins with the termination of the timber trade and shipbuilding in the mid-19th century. Grande Allée, once home to prominent English families, now features restaurants and bars in their former residences. McMahon Street, once the centre of the Irish community, home of St. Patrick's Church and School and the early St. Brigid's Home, now sees these landmarks preserved as historic sites and the people gone elsewhere. The Scottish community centred around St. Andrew's Church, the Kirk School and Morrin College, has scattered, though these sites are still preserved and a section of rue St-Stanislas has been renamed chaussée des Écossais in their memory. Many of the English estates in Sillery are now French-owned residences and institutions run by the government or religious orders.

The ship-builders of Lower Town are gone, as are the bankers of St. Peter Street and the Irish labourers of Petit Champlain. Churches have closed (St. Matthews, Wesley Methodist) and congregations combined and moved to other churches. Quebec High School is fifty percent francophone; St. Lawrence campus of Champlain Regional College is the one English CEGEP; there is no English university. The political climate and the westward drift in search of jobs have also taken their toll.

But, despite its diminishing size, the English community of Quebec City retains its identity and spirit. Protestant and English Catholic churches; schools; cultural organizations such as the "Lit & Hist", the Voice of English-speaking Quebec, the Quebec Art Company and Quebec English Writers' Club; media such as The Quebec Chronicle-Telegraph and CBC Radio's Quebec Community Network; and entities as diverse as Jeffrey Hale's Hospital, St. Brigid's Home and Holland Centre which provide medical and social services for the English community, and Simons clothing store are touchstones of this resolute population. Government-proposed changes in regional administration threatened to swallow up some of these services into the main stream. "The loss of governance of its English-language health care institutions would mean the loss of the community's foundation...." (Michèle Thibeau, *Quebec Chronicle-Telegraph*, March 31, 2004.) Happily, the Quebec City region's Health and Social Services Development Agency has since recommended that Jeffery Hale's Hospital, Saint Brigid's Home and Holland Centre be exempted from the other local service networks. They will be allowed to amalgamate to form a network which will provide services to both the English-speaking and French-speaking populations of the region. The Voice of English-speaking Quebec, one of the participants in the campaign to protect English-language health services, lauds the English and French-speaking residents of Quebec who "joined together to resolve this issue through respectful and reasonable dialogue".

Interesting observations on the experience of being English in Quebec City are offered by longtime residents Diana and Clive Meredith. Diana Meredith, born in England, here since the 1950s, felt a coolness between herself and French-speakers in the 1960s and '70s, but sees a change now, an evolution of confidence on the part of the French. She finds many now anxious to "practice their English" with her. Her husband Clive, a fourth generation Quebecer (his great-grandfather was Chief Justice of Quebec in the mid-19th century) says, "I love Quebec City. I wouldn't move anywhere else, come hell or Sov-Ass!"

The Quebec Chronicle-Telegraph
27 rue Buade.

The Quebec Chronicle-Telegraph claims to be North America's oldest existing newspaper. Its history begins in 1764 with the founding of *The Quebec Gazette* by William Brown. This journal, government-directed in its early years, was published as a weekly until 1832 when it became a bilingual daily, appearing on alternate days in English and French.

In 1847, Robert Middleton founded *The Morning Chronicle*, which in 1873 merged with *The Quebec Gazette* using both names in its title. In 1875, James Carrel started *The Quebec Daily Telegraph*, a liberal publication. Competition forced a merger once again and William Price and James Carrel moved their plant and offices to this building. In 1925, *The Chronicle-Telegraph* emerged. In 1934, the masthead read *The Quebec Chronicle and Telegraph*. The Thompson Company took over in 1959 and moved the operation; as a daily, the paper relied heavily on the wire services; then, in 1972, *The Quebec Chronicle-Telegraph* once again became a weekly.

In 1993, with a seriously shrinking market, the paper was bought by Karen Macdonald and François Vézina. The office is now in their home and the paper is distributed every Wednesday to a circulation of some 1,950.

Local English-language newspapers remain an important tool for the preservation of English and for the dissemination of news of interest to English-speakers in Quebec City and region. A recent issue of *The Quebec Chronicle-Telegraph* had articles on "the bright future" in store for English language health services, plans to celebrate the 200th anniversary of the Anglican cathedral, an editorial supporting the unified city, the commemoration at the "Lit & Hist" of the 90th anniversary of the sinking of the *Empress of Ireland*, a book signing at La Maison Anglaise, and schedules of many classes, religious services and medical assistance available in English. Richard Walling, former manager of the paper, said that "the *Chronicle* is like the glue of the community. It's the vehicle that brings us all together".

The *Chronicle-Telegraph* sign is still visible on the façade of this 1920s building. It is said that if you pass here when the wind is right "you can still smell the ink".

The Cathedral of the Holy Trinity
31 rue des Jardins.

The Anglican Cathedral of the Holy Trinity was built between 1800 and 1804 on the site of the French fur-trading Company of One Hundred Associates. After the Conquest, the Recollets shared their church on this site with the Anglican congregation. On Sunday mornings the English drums would sound a call to service as soon as the Catholic mass was ended. In 1796, the Recollet church burned down and the "English Cathedral" was built here at government expense. It was the first Church of England cathedral ever built outside the British Isles.

The Cathedral is notable for its Royal Pew, set apart in a gallery, to be used only by the sovereign or a representative. King George III donated fabric for an altar frontal which had been used at his coronation at Westminster and gave ten valuable silver altar vessels still in the possession of the Cathedral. Services were attended by Anglicans from the upper strata of Quebec's administrative, military, mercantile and professional groups. Jacob Mountain, Quebec's first Anglican bishop, who is buried in the church, stated that it was "a symbolic statement of English pretensions, powers and privileges". Its size and situation are indicative of the strength and influence of the English in Quebec City at that time. Cathedral archives contain records of births, marriages and burials in the parish dating back to 1766.

Major William Robe and Capt. William Hall of the Royal Artillery designed the Cathedral which they adapted from the Church of St. Martin-in-the-Fields in London, England; most of the stonework and masonry were done by John and Lawrence Cannon, the sons of Irish contractor Edward Cannon. The Palladian style of this cathedral influenced the architecture of many subsequent buildings in the city. Today, it is an historic monument with a small but active congregation.

The Duke of Kent's house
25 rue St-Louis.

The original house on the plot of land in front of this site was occupied in the 1640s by the Governor of New France. Prince Edward, Duke of Kent, later to be father to Queen Victoria, lived here from 1791-94 with Madame de St. Laurent during which time its structure was vastly altered.

It was here in 1759 that General James Murray signed the capitulation of the city with DeRamezay. This historic house was also used as a residence by Bishop Jacob Mountain. Today, it is the French consulate.

The old Union Hotel

12 rue Ste-Anne.

Edward Cannon built well! This Irishman from County Wexford, Ireland was a master mason whose contracting company Edward Cannon & Sons constructed many of Quebec's most prestigious buildings including the jail and this handsome 1805 hotel. He married Eleanor Murphy of St. John's, Newfoundland. Their sons, Ambrose, Lawrence and John, were contractors in the city for many years. In 1808, this building, on Place d'Armes near the Chateau Frontenac, became the meeting place of the bourgeois *Baron's Club*. It was restored in 1964 and is now used as a provincial government tourist bureau.

The Jonathan Sewell house
87 rue St-Louis.

Jonathan Sewell was a prominent citizen when the province of Quebec was called Lower Canada. He was born in Cambridge, Massachusetts in 1766, to a Loyalist judge who would take refuge with his family in Nova Scotia after the American Revolution. Jonathan, who was educated at Oxford, Cambridge and Harvard, came to Quebec in 1789. He was a sound constitutional lawyer who learned to speak fluent French and who became a member of the Legislative Assembly and speaker of the Legislative Council.

He was an important leader of the hated "Château Clique" during the 1830s; an early advocate (1824) of legislative union of the British North American colonies; and a founder of the Literary and Historical Society. He was Chief Justice of Lower Canada during turbulent times, when French Canadians dominated the Assembly and British authorities were suspicious of French revolutionary mobs and of American democracy. This bilingual man who was open to compromise and sympathetic to the Assembly's desires was nonetheless mistrusted by the French because he was Chief Justice and a close advisor to the anti-French Governor Craig. Jonathan Sewell persevered, even throughout the rebellion, and held the post of Chief Justice for thirty years (1808-38). He died in this house in 1839.

Sewell married Henrietta Smith, daughter of Chief Justice William Smith, and fathered sixteen children (one source puts the number at twenty-two and claims that this set a record which held for 100 years). He and his family lived in this house, built in 1803, which stands just inside the St-Louis Gate. The Anglo-American classical style, with its lowered roof pitch, squared stonework and Ionic doorway, marked a new departure in Quebec architecture which emphasized unity, symmetry and order. Its spacious rooms have hosted many events over the years: Sewell family gatherings for joy and for bereavement; political debates and sittings of the Executive Council; and decisions which would affect the future of Canada. In 1854, the Canadian Union government bought the house from the Sewell heirs and employed it for various offices and living quarters. It is now used by the Department of National Defense.

The James Thompson house

47 rue Ste-Ursule.

James Thompson (father of James Gawler Thompson, who became an important judge in the Gaspé, see p.156) was born in Rosshire in the Scottish highlands. He fought at the Battle of the Plains of Abraham in 1759; when he died in 1830, he was the last surviving Fraser Highlander who had fought that day. Thompson was put in charge of Quebec's fortifications. He was a prolific writer, and is often quoted in the history of the Fraser Highlanders.

Some soldiers from this regiment married into the French community; others, like Thompson, into the English. His house, built in 1793, has been beautifully kept and is now a B&B run by Greg Alexander from Toronto. On occasion, local Scots still use the house for ceremonies.

The Citadel

Cape Diamond.

British military engineers planned and built fortifications at Quebec from the last quarter of the 18th century. The chief engineer for the building of the Citadel (1821-30) was Elias Walker Durnford, a colonel in the Royal Engineers, who was influenced by the work of such engineers as Gother Mann and Ralph Bruyère. The Citadel was built in the shape of a star, using the concept of bastions developed by the French military engineer Vauban, creating what came to be called the "Gibraltar of America".

The Citadel was built of limestone from Cap Rouge atop the much weaker French fortifications. The limestone blocks were transported to the site by boat and by ox-cart, and winched up a 360-foot ramp at a 45-degree angle from the river using horse power. Many of the craftsmen who worked on the Citadel came from the Quebec City garrison, including some German mercenaries. In 1828 there were eight hundred and seventy-three craftsmen and day labourers on the site.

The main threat to the city at this time was seen to be from the Americans. Attempts at invasion in 1775-76 and 1812-14 were not successful. There was also the fear that France might set her sights on re-capturing Quebec. The Citadel was, in fact, never tested, but perhaps served as a deterrent.

When the British withdrew their garrison in 1871, the fortifications were taken over by the Canadian government. Quebec citizens began using its stones to build their houses until Governor-General Dufferin rescued the walls and had two gates rebuilt. Quebec is, in fact, the only city in North America to have preserved the major portion of its walled city.

Since 1920, the Citadel has been the home of Canada's renowned French-Canadian regiment The Royal 22nd ("Van Doos"). It serves as the residence of Canada's Governor-General when she or he visits Quebec City.

Martello I
Battlefields Park.

Battlefields Park was created to commemorate two battles: the battle of the Plains of Abraham in 1759, won by the English; and the Battle of Ste-Foy in 1760, won by the French. In 1908, landscape architect Frederick Todd, who designed many parks throughout the province of Quebec including Victoria Park in Granby, was hired to design this park. It was originally named the "Plains of Abraham" after Abraham Martin, the King's pilot, who grazed his cattle here.

With an increasing threat of American invasion in the early 19th century, British engineers built sixteen Martello towers as part of their fortifications for British North America. Three still stand in Quebec.

The word Martello is an English corruption of Mortella, a point in Corsica where such a tower had so impressed British forces that they built two hundred of them throughout their empire. The cleverness of the design lay in the fact that, if taken by the enemy, they could be destroyed by cannon-fire from the rear. This result was assured by building the side of the tower facing the town with thinner walls.

Martello tower I, overlooking the St. Lawrence River, was erected in 1812 to protect the main fortifications. Covered in sandstone, it has limited openings well off the ground. The entrance stands at a height two and a half times that of a 19th century man. It was reached by a removable ladder.

The Garrison Club
Rue St-Louis and rue d'Auteuil.

In the foreground of this photo stands the St-Louis Gate, a part of the walled city, which was designed by William Lynn, a Belfast-trained architect from County Wexford who also designed the St. John's Gate. The first St-Louis Gate was built in 1692 by Governor Frontenac. During Lord Dufferin's term in the 1870s, these French medieval-style gates replaced the British military fortification gates which had allowed passage of only one horse-drawn vehicle at a time. Beyond the gate we see the building erected in 1816 as the headquarters of the Royal Engineers.

The British army left Canada in 1871, and in 1879 Canadian militia officers founded the Garrison Club, the oldest military club in Canada. It operated at these premises in the tradition of British private clubs, both civil and military, as a social and recreational facility. The Garrison Club and the Chateau Frontenac Hotel were for many years favourite gathering places for the English of Quebec City. The Garrison is now a private club which merged some time ago with Le Cercle Universitaire, and is now known as Le Cercle de la Garnison Québec/Garrison Club. The garden, with trees over 125-years old, is one of the most beautiful in Quebec City.

St. Andrew's Presbyterian Church

Corner of rue Ste-Anne and Cook.

St. Andrew's has been home to the oldest English-speaking congregation of Scottish origin in Canada. The present site was granted by King George III in 1802 and the church, designed by architect John Bryson, was built in 1810 opposite the jail which would become Morrin College. The Celtic Cross is part of the interior decor of this church which was built according to the traditions of Scottish Presbyterian kirks. It remains almost unchanged except for the stained glass windows which were a later addition. Flags of the Cross of St. Andrew, the Fraser and Cameron Highlanders and the Union Jack decorate the walls.

Quebec City Scots were prominent in the administration and development of the city; the congregation of the Church of Scotland, which included soldiers of the 78th Fraser Highlanders in Wolfe's army and merchants from Scotland and New England, has worshipped in Quebec City since 1759. Prior to the building of this church they held their services in the chapel of the Ursulines and the Jesuit's College. Attendance at Sunday service today averages about twenty, few of whom are locals.

Kirk Hall
Chausée des Écossais

Built in 1829, this is one of the oldest existing English school buildings in Quebec City. It stands near St. Andrew's Church from whose congregation it drew its students. The St. Andrew's Society, which provided assistance to needy Scots immigrants, especially in the Eastern Townships, held its meetings in Kirk Hall before it moved to Morrin College circa 1868. Kirk Hall was used as a school until 1885 when it became a minister's residence; in 1909, it became a community hall and home to a Sunday school.

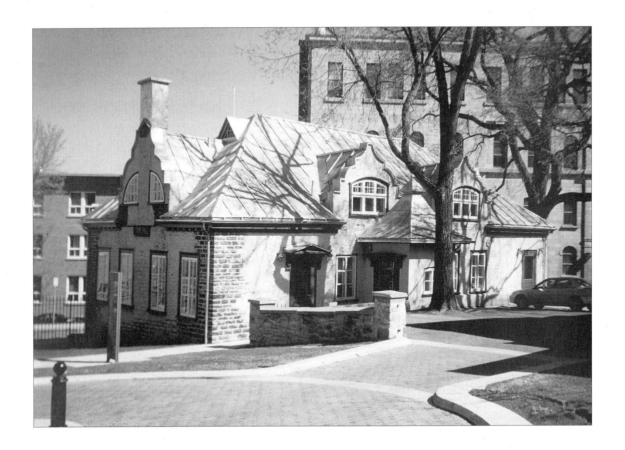

The Morrin College building
44 chausée des Écossais.

This Paladian building was designed circa 1808 by architect François Baillairgé and erected by contractor Edward Cannon and his sons John and Lawrence. It was the first

prison in Canada which put into practice the principles of John Howard, a British reformer, who believed that confinement in cells, work and education could rehabilitate criminals. But, by the 1860s, overcrowding and vandalism had rendered this building unusable as a prison and it was sold. The last public hanging in Quebec was held here in 1864.

Dr. Joseph Morrin, Scottish-born mayor of Quebec City (1855-58) , said to have been "the first freely elected mayor" of that city, and founder of the College of Physicians and Surgeons of Lower Canada, bought this former prison in 1868. He established a Presbyterian college for the training of young men for the ministry and the education of young women in the liberal arts. Morrin College operated for half a century, but ultimately declined as the majority of English-speaking Quebecers preferred to send their children to study at McGill University. During his tenure Dr. Morrin provided space for the Literary and Historical Society of Quebec where it remains to this day.

The "Lit and Hist" was created as a learned society in 1824, the first of its kind in North America. Among its founders were Lord Dalhousie, Jonathan Sewell and French Canada's first historian, François-Xavier Garneau. Its mandate was to collect and make public artifacts and documents related to the earliest history of Canada, especially those pertaining to the First Nations.

Among its achievements: an 1841 petition by the Society, with the Natural History Society of Montreal, which led to the founding of the Geological Survey of Canada; a petition in 1871 which led to the founding of the National Archives in Ottawa; and the hosting of many international luminaries, among them Charles Dickens.

Though its francophone membership has stood at about one-third since its founding, the society was regarded from the beginning with suspicion. Members of the Legislative Assembly suspected that the colonial administrators were using it to "appropriate history and define culture".

The "Lit and Hist" houses the only English library in Quebec City. With about two hundred and fifty members and a budget of $50,000, it survives on little government money, income from ancient investments, donations, subscriptions and the kindness of friends: a retired bookbinder takes home damaged books and restores them; the clock was repaired free of charge by the grandson of the original clockmaker. Despite these constraints, no fines are ever levied for late books.

A new role for the historic building is in the works. The goal is full restoration of its facilities and the creation of an English language cultural venue to be called 'Morrin Centre'. Here, special events, lectures and discussions will illuminate various aspects of Quebec's English history and culture.

The National School
Rue d'Auteuil at rue Dauphine.

In 1819, the Quebec branch of the British Society for the Promotion of Christian Knowledge opened a National School for poor children of all Christian denominations in the Hope Gate Guard House at the foot of Ste-Famille St. The students soon moved to this building erected in 1823. In its early days the National School educated the sons and daughters of soldiers as well as "deaf-mutes and orphans" in reading, writing and arithmetic. In 1827, the school was "in a flourishing condition" and was attended by 125 boys and 105 girls, about two-thirds of whom belonged to the Church of England. Later, only boys were educated here.

In the 1880s, this building was used by the Anglican churches to run their Sunday schools and in the 20th century it was sold to the Jesuits. Louisa Blair, a Quebec City historian, pointed out that "while in its heyday temperance was one of the subjects taught in the building, in recent history it has achieved renown as the home of a well loved nightclub and bar." It is now undergoing extensive renovations.

St. Patrick's Church
9 McMahon Street.

In 1832, there were about 8,000 Irish living in Quebec City. Immigrants of the 1820s, not the famine years of the 1840s, were the founders of the Quebec Irish community. From 1817, these English-speakers, who wished to have a ministry in their language, had been petitioning Bishop Plessis for a church of their own. French authorities were opposed to the idea, but, after years of struggle and negotiation, they finally approved the building of an Irish church. The cornerstone was laid in 1832 and the first Mass was said in 1833 in this, the first Irish Catholic church in Canada.

Father Patrick McMahon, from Abbeyleix, Ireland, was the chaplain of St. Patrick's until 1851. In addition to the large Irish population of the city, the church served the local garrison; many Irish serving in the British army were married here. The architect was Thomas Baillairgé; the remaining walls are the only standing vestiges of his work in Quebec City. The first pipe organ, installed in 1837, was donated by Protestants who collected funds to purchase it in England. Calixa Lavallée, composer of the music for *O Canada*, was one of St. Patrick's organists.

The church closed in 1959 after the congregation had moved on to a new St. Patrick's on Grande Allée. A fire destroyed much of this church in 1970. The front facade, seen here, was saved and a new structure added which has become a cancer research centre operated by l'Hôtel-Dieu de Québec.

The building of St. Patrick's Church in 1832 was a momentous event for the Irish of Quebec City, recognizing as it did their existence as a community.

St. Patrick's School
10 McMahon Street.

This was the first school specifically for Irish boys in Quebec City. It was started in 1842 by the Brothers of the Christian Schools, both French and English, and very shortly after that was named St. Patrick's School. St. Patrick's changed locations in the early years. This building was erected circa 1880; an extra floor was added later. Irish boys were educated here until 1918 when a new school was opened on De Salaberry Street "in the suburbs".

Before Bill 22, St. Patrick's High School had some 1,400 students. By 1980 that number had fallen to 673. Principal William McNamara said at the time, "I don't know where the survival (of the English) is going to come from if they are leaving this way."

This building is now known as l'Édifice McMahon, a research centre for l'Hôtel-Dieu de Québec.

Saint Brigid's Home
corner of St-Stanislas and McMahon (Artillery Park).

"The Home" as it is still called, was created in the mid-19th century to care for homeless Irish children, widows and elderly. Famine, disease and poverty had afflicted many who were in need of help.

Father James Nelligan raised funds from the garrison soldiers to build a children's home. His successor, Father Bernard McGauran, carried on his work and rented space here (the site is disputed) as a shelter for women and children. The first matron was Mary Ann Bradley (1856-58); the Grey Nuns then ran the home until 1944 when the Sisters of Charity of Halifax took over.

The home was named St. Bridget's until 1973 when it moved from Grande Allée to Sillery and the spelling was changed to "Brigid", considered to be more Irish. Saint Brigid's still operates in Sillery, now serving English and French, Protestant and Catholic.

The Celtic Cross in the foreground is dedicated: "to the people of Quebec from the people of Ireland in remembrance of their selfless compassion in time of need."

Dinan's Hill street sign

Côte Dinan.

Frank Dinan, from an Irish family still prominent in Quebec City, was a long-serving alderman. In addition to politics, the family contributed to the economic and educational life of the city. This street was named in recognition of their beneficence.

The High School of Quebec   *30 rue St-Denis.*

This school served the English Protestant community for one hundred years (1842-1941). It was referred to as the "Old Quebec High School"; girls went to Commissioners High School, which no longer exists. The church-like section with the large Gothic window was the gymnasium. Later, this became an elementary school for both boys and girls. Going to school here could be a chilly proposition; Marion Blinco, a student here in its later years, remembers the "frost on the pipes".

Protestant students, both boys and girls – separated, of course – moved to the new Quebec High School on rue Belvédère in 1942. Part of the Central Quebec School Board, it still educates English students, though declining enrolment is a concern. The school population is now fifty per cent francophone, thanks to the use of the "grandfather clause" of Bill 101, whereby French-speaking children who have a parent or grandparent who was educated in English in Quebec may attend an English school.

There is no English university in Quebec City, although l'Université de Laval does permit English students to write exams in their own language (there is an agreement among Quebec universities, both French and English, to allow students to submit their work in either official language). Lack of employment in English, the absence of an English university and the political climate have all contributed to an exodus of young English-speakers from Quebec City.

Simons store

20 côte de la Fabrique.

The Simons family have been merchants in Quebec City for over one hundred and sixty years. In 1840, John Simons set up shop on St. John Street, just inside the gate. His father, Peter, came to Quebec City from Scotland. He had fought with Nelson at the Battle of the Nile where he sustained an eye infection; his retirement package was a small seigniory at Lake Beauport.

John Simons stocked his dry-goods store with merchandise ordered from a cousin in Scotland. His son Archibald, in his turn, made over forty buying trips to Britain. The store moved to these premises (the building on the left) in the 1860s. They later acquired the building on the right from Birks.

In 1937, a women's clothing section was added. Under Archibald's grandson Donald and Donald's sons Peter and Richard, the business has expanded throughout the province of Quebec to Ste-Foy, Sherbrooke, Montreal and Laval. The head office is still here. Donald remains in charge of corporate business and is the secretary, while Peter and Richard run the stores' operations.

Donald Simons says that the key to their success has been in merchandising. Simons offers products from all over the world: men's and women's clothing, Irish linens, Scottish woollens and so forth. Occasionally a problem arises over the use of English terms in their advertising, but since the stores operate in French, Donald Simons says that there has been no friction between the English owner and French employees.

The Wesley Church
Dauphine and St-Stanislas.

This lovely church, one of the finest neo-Gothic churches in Quebec, was built in 1848. Inside, there is a monument to Pierre Langlois (1784-1864), from Guernsey, one of the pioneers of Methodism in Quebec.

In 1931, the shrinking congregation here joined Chalmers Presbyterian Church to form Chalmers-Wesley United Church. In 1944, Sen. Lorne C. Webster and his family donated this building to the city which restored it in 1948. It is now home to the Institut Canadien.

The Institut Canadien was formed in the 1840s by a group of young professionals who were inspired by the writings of French and British liberals. New ideas from Europe had reached Quebec. The Institut encouraged free thought, libraries, democracy and national feelings. They welcomed people of all languages and faiths. Many such groups were established throughout the province, but were hindered by the powerful and conservative Catholic Church.

Now, this former Protestant church is home to a francophone institute which is free from the constraints of the Church. Among those who have addressed its members was the late Mordecai Richler.

The Chalmers Presbyterian Church
78 rue Ste-Ursule.

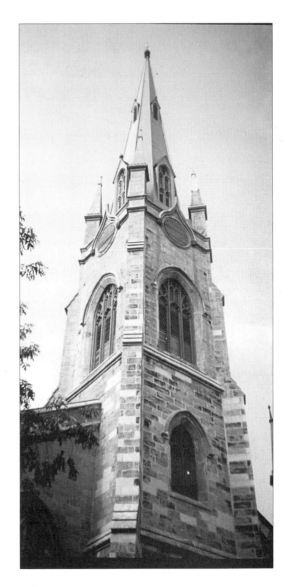

The congregation of this church has existed for two hundred years. St. John's Presbyterian congregation built this neo-Gothic church in 1853, naming it Chalmers Presbyterian after Thomas Chalmers, leader of the Free Church movement in Scotland. It has the tallest steeple in Old Quebec.

In 1931, the Wesley Methodist congregation joined Chalmers to form the Chalmers-Wesley United Church. Stained glass from the old Wesley Church, designed by W. J. Fisher at the Leonard workshop in Old Quebec, was installed here. Since 1987, this church has shared its space with a French Protestant congregation, Église Unie St-Pierre.

A legendary story connected to this church is that of the Gavazzi riots in its first year of existence. Gavazzi was a renegade Catholic priest who preached against the Church and, as such, was welcomed in Protestant churches. When he began a sermon at Chalmers, an Irish crowd threw rocks at the windows, Gavazzi fled, and the Irish, satisfied, returned home to celebrate.

The Jeffrey Hale's Hospital
250 boulevard René-Lévesque.

The original Jeffrey Hale's Hospital was built on rue Saint-Olivier in 1865 to serve the Protestant English population of the city. It had fifteen beds and stood in a good location in Upper Town, with a view of the river and countryside, away from the unsanitary parts of the city. By 1900, that building had become too small and, in 1901, this one in the château style seen throughout the city was constructed to replace it. The McKenzie Memorial building, 300 René-Lévesque, was added to the complex in 1906.

Jeffrey Hale Hospital in the 19st century

Jeffrey Hale, son of a British soldier, was born in Quebec City in 1803 and educated in England. He joined the Royal Navy where he rose to the rank of captain. After leaving the navy, he served as Receiver-General of Canada. He was a man of social conscience who, in his will, left 9,000 pounds sterling for the building of the hospital that would bear his name. Religion was long ago dropped as a requirement for admission.

The hospital moved its premises again, in the 1950s, to chemin Ste-Foy. This building is now a specialized hospital which shares its facilities with francophones. Many English-speaking Quebecers were born in one of these Jeffrey Hale's Hospitals. Today, the Jeffrey Hale Pavilion houses the offices of The Voice of English Quebec and Holland Centre.

Jeffrey Hale Pavilion as it is today.

St. Matthew's Church and cemetery

St. John Street.

A "rightful" king of England is buried in this cemetery. So goes the saga of Robert Wood, son of Prince Edward, Duke of Kent and Madame de St-Laurent. The Duke served in Quebec in the 1790s and fathered a son while he was here. He was subsequently summoned home by King George III and set the task of siring the next monarch. Queen Victoria was his daughter. Robert, meanwhile, was left behind to be brought up by the Duke's batman.

Robert, who was eventually adopted in Quebec City, went on to marry and to grandfather William Wood who wrote a series of history books on Canada. William was apparently accorded special treatment by the Royal Family, lending credence to the story of his lineage. And, on a darker note, it is alleged that Robert is buried here in an unmarked grave, apparently on the orders of Queen Victoria (his half-sister!) A local historian claims to have found the grave, but will not reveal its location.

This cemetery, considered to be the oldest in Quebec, was used from 1772 to 1860. In the 1847 cholera outbreak, there were six hundred and fifty-two victims in Quebec City one hundred and sixty of whom were Protestant. Several of these are buried here. A little funeral chapel was replaced by a church which was destroyed by fire in 1845. This splendid church, whose architect was William T. Thomas, was built between 1870 and 1882 and was consecrated in 1892. Previously, small congregations met in houses until they grew large enough to warrant a church. The now decreasing numbers have resulted in many closures, including this one in 1979. The congregation has merged with St. Michael's in Sillery – now, St. Michael's and St. Matthew's.

St. Matthew's was sold to the city for one dollar and in 1980 became a municipal library. Original plaques still adorn the walls of the library, including some commemorating those killed in both World Wars.

The churchyard is a green oasis in this busy part of the city. In addition to Robert Wood (possibly), others interred here include Capt. Thomas Scott (1823), younger brother of Sir Walter Scott, and Thomas Dunn, a member of the first British Executive Council of Quebec, which had been formed in 1764. Canon Frederick George Scott, the renowned World War I cleric, ended his career at this church.

The Quebec City YMCA
Place Youville.

The English were influential in bringing leisure activities to the people of Quebec: golf, curling, fly-fishing, tennis, etc. English Protestants also fostered a playground association to address the lack of play space for children. The English sport of football has become popular in Quebec City schools and at the university level, illustrated by the success of Laval's *Rouge et Or* and great fan support.

The YMCA sign is still visible on this 1873 building where young English people once participated in "Y" activities. YMCA facilities moved to other locations and have recently closed. This building is now occupied by shops. The YWCA still operates, with a mainly francophone clientele.

The Capitol Theatre

Place Youville.

This early 20th century movie house is currently a French dinner theatre with hotel rooms above.

In 1916, rioters opposed to conscription occupied the War Department offices on the upper floors. They threw typewriters and the contents of filing cabinets out the windows. The cavalry galloped through St. John's Gate to crush the riot, only to be tripped by piano wire strung across the street. The Quebec City police, led by the Walsh brothers, had difficulty controlling the crowd. Many were injured and some were killed.

The Sir William Price residence
145 Grande Allée.

William Price, later Sir William, carried on the entrepreneurial spirit of the Price family. He realized that the pulp and paper industry would eventually eclipse the "senior service" – lumber – and developed his enterprise accordingly.

He considered his company to be part of "la famille Price" and took pride in providing fair wages and proper treatment for his workers, in whom he was said to have taken a personal interest by such actions as the sending of wedding gifts and funeral wreaths and coming personally to honour workers who had served him for fifty years. Sir William had also served as an MP from 1908 to 1912; endowed a chair in chemistry at l'Université de Laval; and raised a regiment for service in the Great War.

This house, built circa 1900, is situated on Grande Allée where many other prominent English families, with names such as Carter, Meredith and Blair, lived. It later became home to the Quebec Renaissance Club patronized by the Union Nationale Party of Premier Maurice Duplessis and is now a restaurant/bar (as are many of its neighbours).

The Ladies' Protestant Home
Grande Allée at Cartier.

Jeffrey Hale was one of the supporters of this institution, incorporated in 1859, which was founded to provide a home for the "friendless and destitute women and female children of the Protestant poor of Quebec". Ronnie Blair, whose family members are long-time Quebec City residents, reminisced about his grandmother – older at the time than most of the residents – reading to the ladies and violating the rules by smuggling in an occasional bottle of beer for one who was particularly fond of it.

In later years, fewer and fewer women qualified for entry under the original terms and the Home began to accept paying residents. When not enough women applied, men were accepted. One of the first men to live there was Edward Montefiore Joseph, a distinguished Jew of the English-speaking community. Ronnie Blair remarked on the drollness of a Jewish man living at the Ladies Protestant Home. Another prominent Quebecer, Hilly Gibaut, a pillar of the Anglican Cathedral, ended his days here.

In the late 1980s, this building, which had opened in 1863, was converted into residences when the Ladies' Protestant Home closed its doors. Nineteen of the remaining thirty-six residents were accepted into St. Brigid's at their premises in Sillery.

The Henry/Stuart house
Grande Allée at Cartier.

Entrepreneur Joseph Archer built this house in 1849-50 for Maria Curry, wife of wood merchant William Henry. In 1918 it became the property of Mary and Adele Stuart, great-granddaughters of author Phillipe Aubert de Gaspé and of prominent Quebec City lawyer Andrew Stuart. Adele, who created a charming garden and was renowned for her tea parties, died here in 1987 at the age of 98.

The Quebec government took over this historic cottage in 1988 and made it the head-quarters of "Le Conseil des Monuments et Sites du Québec". In 1990, the house, furniture (some of which remains) and gardens were classed as "biens culturels" by the Department of Cultural Affairs which now offers guided tours of the premises.

The Clarendon Hotel

Rue Ste-Anne.

Another hotel once stood on this site which stands across the street from the Anglican cathedral. It was frequented, when Parliament was in session, by politicians such as John A. Macdonald and D'Arcy McGee. This hotel, designed by architect Charles Baillairgé, was built in 1866.

The Clarendon's restaurant, named for the architect of the building, boasts of being the "oldest restaurant in Canada", and the Clarendon Hotel of being the oldest in Quebec City. In the dining room and reception area are many historic photographs of the city's past. In one, an early photo of the Clarendon when it stood opposite a park, we see a unilingual English sign which reads "Keep Off the Grass".

41

Price House
Rue Ste-Anne.

The cornerstone of this Art Deco building, Quebec City's first skyscraper, was laid on Black Tuesday, October 29, 1929. It was built for the Price Brothers Paper Company for one million dollars, commissioned by the heirs of Sir William. The Depression and questionable investments, on the heels of this huge expenditure, cost the Price family control of the company. No longer dominant on Quebec City's skyline, this building can still be seen from Lévis and Île d'Orléans.

Once a leading English commercial centre, Price House was acquired in 2000 as the head office of the Caisse de Dêpot et Placement du Québec, whose responsibility it is to invest Quebec's large public-sector pension and insurance funds. Now called l'Édifice Price, it once boasted among its tenants the Premier of Quebec, Bernard Landry, who had his official residence and offices here on the upper floors.

In an alcove next to the building stands a monument honouring the lumberjacks of the Saguenay. There is no mention of "le Père du Saguenay", William Price, who developed the lumber business in that region.

The James Hunt store
58-60 St. Peter Street (rue St-Pierre).

The concentration of financial institutions on St. Peter Street earned it the nickname "Wall Street of Quebec". It was, at one time, the financial centre of Lower Canada, with four banks, including the Bank of Montreal and John Woolsey's Quebec Bank (1818), serving the timber trade. The Quebec Stock Exchange (1818) and many insurance companies also had their offices here.

This building, with living quarters above, was designed by architect J. F. Peachey in 1863 for James Hunt. Pictured are the bas reliefs above the windows of James Hunt's store. Three of the four are of classical figures, but the one on the left seems to be sporting a businessman's hat of the time.

The London Coffee House
50 rue du Marché Champlain.

Originally the Hôtel Chevalier (1752), this building continued to be used for commercial purposes under the British regime. It was bought by George Pozer in 1807 and rented to an innkeeper who inscribed London Coffee House on its façade. The photo shows the back of the inn which faced the river. The guests included ships' captains, travelers and businessmen from St. Peter Street. An advertisement of the time read:

"Conveniences for the businessmen – proximity to steam-boat landings, banks, splendid view.
The table: chocolate, delicacies of the season, Wines, liqueurs, cigars.
Beds under superintendence of Mrs. Melrose.
The charges will be moderate."

The name London Coffee House was retained into the early 20th century. The inn and surrounding buildings were restored in the 1960s, maintaining their Quebec architectural heritage. Today, they are known as Maison Chevalier, managed by La Musée de la Civilization, and house an interpretation centre which holds thematic exhibitions.

Hayden's Wexford House
450 rue Champlain ("The Cove").

Dating from 1832, this was an inn when the port of Quebec was bustling with sailors, travelers and raftsmen who transported the timber rafts from as far away as Fort Coulonge on the Ottawa River, through the Lake of Two Mountains, to the coves of Quebec City where they were loaded onto ships bound for Britain.

Rue Champlain, Lower Town, was an Irish enclave, home to the struggling Irish who worked as stevedores and in other labouring jobs. Cheap houses built next to the cliffs were sometimes the victims of deadly rock-slides which took lives and destroyed buildings. It was here, in 1862, that one of Canada's first labour unions was formed. The Quebec Shiplabourer's Benevolent Society protected stevedores from dishonest ships' captains and gave financial support to workers' families during times of illness and injury. In 2003, the Toponomy Committee recommended that a street in Quebec City be named after Richard Burke, from County Wexford, one of the charter members of this society.

Today, Hayden's Wexford House is a B&B. Part of rue Champlain, called rue du Petit Champlain, has been extensively renovated. Its boutiques and restaurants and cobbled car-free road are a mecca for tourists. This end of the street more accurately reflects its past

Number 6 Fire-station
428-436 rue Champlain.

18th century Britain had outlawed the Irish tongue and most of the Irish immigrants arrived here speaking English, many having lost all knowledge of their own language. The Irish played an important role in this city: in municipal politics, in the Church, as lawyers, as builders, as a large percentage of the dock labour and as policemen and firemen.

This was Number 6 fire-station in the heart of Irish Quebec City. Visible on the upper façade is the number "6" surrounded by shamrocks. In that era of mud roads and horse-drawn fire-wagons, its motto was, "Faugh-a-Balla" – clear the way. The building is now divided into dwellings. The photo was taken from the facing street, rue des Sapeurs (firemen).

The Customs House

130 Dalhousie Street, Pointe-à-Carcy Promenade.

The customs office, dating back to 1762, was one of the first British civic institutions established in Quebec. This grey-stone building with splendid Italianate columns, facing the St. Lawrence River, was designed by William Thomas and built in 1851. It was later decorated by William Lynn, one of the many artisans brought to the city by Lord Dufferin. The figures above the windows are modeled on those which grace the Ulster Bank.

Quebec City, at this time, held a dominant place in shipbuilding and in the timber trade. A British law prohibiting the purchase of American-made ships encouraged Scottish and English shipbuilders to come to Quebec. Beatson, Munn, Goudie, Russell, Bell, Davie, Taylor, Black, Wood, Menzies and Dinning are among their names.

The Customs House and Trinity House are situated in Lower Town near the ship-yards. John Munn built the *Jeannie Johnston* here in 1847. She was a timber ship, exemplary in the treatment accorded the Irish immigrants who came on her return voyages to Canada. She made sixteen crossings between 1848 and 1856. Unusually for these ships, she had a medical officer on board. No passenger died aboard the *Jeannie Johnston,* the only ship on this route to hold such a record. A replica of this ship sailed to Quebec City in 2003. The *Royal William*, built in Quebec City by James Goudie who learned his trade at Greenock, Scotland, was the first steamboat to cross the Atlantic entirely under steam.

Before 1759, there was a French ship-building industry along the St. Charles River. After the Conquest, these yards were taken over and run by experts from Scotland and England. They employed thousands of men, capitalizing on the craftsmanship of the French workers and employing the Irish in the rigging trade.

Under the aegis of these entrepreneurs, Quebec City became one of the great ship-building cities in British North America. Alison Davie would later establish a yard across the river at Lévis. The Davie shipyard is now the oldest continuously operating yard in North America. The shipyards of Lower Town have disappeared, but the tradition survives with Davie at Lévis.

Trinity House
150 Dalhousie Street, Pointe-à-Carcy Promenade.

Annual port traffic in Quebec City grew from about one hundred ships in 1790 to over two thousand in 1830. In the mid-19th century, Quebec stood fifth in the world for tonnage in its port. The timber trade was in high gear, supplying the British navy and, at home, providing building materials for the ever-increasing immigrant population. Farms produced wheat for export and manufactured items such as textiles, machinery and household goods arrived from Britain.

Trinity House was established in 1805 to maintain control of the port and the timber ships, steamboats, fishing craft and barges who used her facilities.

For decades, the wardens of Trinity House regulated this traffic with pilots' licenses, lights and buoys and investigation of infractions.

The Promenade was built on reclaimed land. Private wharves were constructed and the first deep-water wharf was built by James Goudie at the foot of rue St-Antoine. In 1888, many of the duties of Trinity House were transferred to the Quebec Harbour Commission. In 1913-14, this handsome building, the new Trinity House, which features a clock tower, was constructed. Today, it houses the Quebec Port Authority. Employees, when asked, had never heard the name Trinity House.

Palace Station
Rue de la Gare.

This CPR station, designed by architect Edward Prindle in the French chateau style, was built in 1915. It stands on the site of Quebec's royal shipyard during the French régime and near the site of George Taylor's shipyard in the early 19th century. Taylor joined forces with his son-in-law Alison Davie in this enterprise in 1825. Today, this is a bus station and home to the VIA Rail terminus and offices.

The Château Frontenac *1 rue des Carrières.*

The Château Frontenac has dominated the skyline of Quebec City and been its emblem for over one hundred years. It was built in 1893 for the CPR, whose General Manager William Van Horne hired architect Bruce Price of New York to design this neo-Gothic structure. Price, who was the father of manners authority Emily Post, also designed Windsor Station in Montreal.

The hotel was built in phases between 1893 and 1924 and now boasts 613 rooms and suites, many public rooms and Dufferin Terrace. This was named for Governor-General Lord Dufferin who was responsible for the construction of the terrace (1873-78), which from its elevation of two hundred feet offers strollers a view across the St. Lawrence to Lévis. Kiosks which dot the terrace are named for members of the British Royal family such as Queen Victoria and Princess Louise.

The Château is built on the site of Château Haldimand, residence of British Governors from 1784 to 1860, and near the site of the Château St. Louis, home to the French Governors. The Swiss-born Haldimand, who spoke French better than he spoke English, was Governor of Quebec from 1778 to 1786. In 1943 and 1944, Prime Minister Mackenzie King hosted President Franklin D. Roosevelt and Prime Minister Winston Churchill here to discuss strategy in the war against Germany and Japan.

The Château Frontenac is today a five-star hotel attracting visitors worldwide.

"Bishopthorpe"
69 rue D'Auteuil.

This handsome Italianate building, whose exterior remains virtually unchanged, was, over a period of years, the residence of four of Quebec's Anglican bishops. It was built in the late 19th century by Thomas McGreevy who was also the contractor for the Canadian Parliament buildings.

The Winter Club
650 Laurier Avenue.

This clubhouse was built, in the 1920s, and supported by the English Protestant community. In the 1940s and 1950s, it was the only venue which offered swimming lessons in the city. Other activities here included: badminton, curling, and other indoor winter activities.

The decline of the English population here led to the eventual closing of the Winter Club. The YMCA used the building for awhile, but it too closed. Now the owner is the Chateau Laurier Hotel which stands next door. Rumour has it that the plan is to demolish the building and create a car park.

The Beth Israel Ohev Shalom Synagogue

DeSalaberry at Crémazie.

Quebec City Jews, mostly bilingual, have long been part of the English community here. Their relatively small numbers (the 1851 census listed 181 Jews in Montreal, while only forty in Quebec City) made it difficult for the congregation to build a synagogue. Only in 1892 was the first permanent synagogue, the Beth Israel, built.

Despite their small numbers, the Jewish community of Quebec City fostered some prominent citizens: Abraham Joseph, who settled in Quebec in 1832, became the President of the Quebec Board of Trade and a city councillor; Sigismund Mohr, who came to Canada in 1871, is considered by some to have been the "father of hydro-electricity" in Canada. He introduced the latest innovations of his day – the telephone and electric lighting; and John Franks was the chief of the Quebec fire brigade between 1790 and 1799.

This synagogue was built in 1944 and suffered a suspicious fire soon after, which some attributed to Vichy sympathizers who were quite influential in the city. With a declining congregation and financial difficulties in the 1970s, the decision was made to sell the building in 1980. The tiny community (one hundred in 2002) now uses a modest building on De Mérici Avenue for its synagogue.

This building on DeSalaberry, after a considerable re-modeling and some additions, houses the Théatre Periscope.

"Kilmarnock"
1479a rue Negabamat, Sillery.

This land, reaching all the way to the St. Lawrence River, was once the Fief de Monceaux. In 1785, Murdock Stuart bought the domain and, at the end of the 18th century, sold it to John McNider, a Quebec City merchant. The old Manoir de Monceaux was in ruins and was demolished around that time.

This stone house, built by McNider circa 1800 and named *Kilmarnock* after his native village in Scotland, is said to be the oldest in Sillery. Descendants of the McNiders lived here in the 19th century. The domain, sub-divided into many lots, is now part of a large development of expensive homes. This house is now called Manoir Kilmarnok [*sic*].

Mount Hermon cemetery   *1801 chemin St-Louis, Sillery.*

The major epidemics of cholera, typhoid and smallpox were a constant concern in Quebec City with its ever-increasing immigrant population. It was believed that the badly maintained cemeteries in the city were a source of these diseases. In 1855, the government passed legislation forbidding further burials in the city's cemeteries and requiring them to be performed three miles outside the city limits. Cemeteries would now be developed in the country.

The Quebec Protestant Cemetery Association was formed in 1848 (the same year as the Mount Royal Cemetery in Montreal), the first suburban cemetery in the region. It bought the property of Judge Edwards which stood just south of the Fief Saint-Michel. The first president of the Association was George Okill Stuart, a lawyer who was mayor of Quebec (1846) and a member of the Legislative Assembly. Named Mount Hermon after the mountain in northern Israel, this is a garden cemetery – 26 acres of trees, bushes and paths with a view of the river – landscaped by Major David Bates Douglass, a professor who had designed cemeteries in New York State. The first burial here took place on June 15, 1848.

The Treggett family, beginning with William Treggett, have supervised the cemetery since 1865. The present superintendent, Brian Treggett, has run it since 1966. In his care are more than 16,000 gravesites. Among the many prominent English citizens of Quebec City buried here are: William Price ("le Père du Saguenay"); George Davie (shipbuilding); Christian Wurtele (photographer); and Dr. James Douglas (Beauport Asylum).

"Cataraqui"

2141 chemin St-Louis, Sillery.

The sprawling mansion and adjacent farm buildings of this large estate were constructed in several stages in the 19th century. Those who lived here included J.B. Forsyth, a merchant, in the early 1830s, and Henry Burstall, a relative of Forsyth and also a merchant, who hired Edward Staveley to re-design and re-construct the house. After the fire at *Spencer Wood* in 1860, *Cataraqui* became the residence of the Governor of Lower Canada, Sir Edmund Head.

Many owners and changes ensued: Charles Levey (1863); Geoffrey Rhodes (1905); and Rhodes' daughter, Catherine, who was married to the painter Henry Percyval Tudor-Hart and lived here until her death in 1972. During this period, part of the mansion served as Tudor-Hart's studio until his death in 1954.

The spacious grounds were developed by Scottish landscape architect M. P. Lowe and a conservatory, which preserved exotic plants, was added. In 1976, the government of Quebec acquired the property and opened it to the public as a garden museum *Domaine Cataraqui*.

The Bishop Mountain School
2046 chemin St-Louis, Sillery.

This stone chapel was built in 1864 on the grounds of Saint Michael's Church and named for Bishop George J. Mountain who served as the third Anglican Bishop of Quebec from 1838 to 1863. Bishop Mountain, whose father had been the first Anglican bishop of Quebec, was renowned for his treks, sometimes on foot, throughout his vast diocese which included the Gaspé and the Magdalen Islands.

The chapel later became a school and now houses the offices of the Central Quebec School Board which is responsible for English schools in an area covering Jonquière, Shawinigan, Thetford Mines, Three Rivers and Quebec City.

"Spencer Grange"
1328 rue Duquet, Sillery.

The many large estates created by English-speakers in Sillery owe their existence to the success of the timber trade and other commercial undertakings which garnered great wealth in the first half of the 19th century. *Spencer Grange* was built by Henry Atkinson in 1849. Families prided themselves in owning mansions such as this with well-designed English-style gardens and well-tended forests.

Some of the owners of *Spencer Grange* who succeeded Henry Atkinson were: his son-in-law James MacPherson Lemoine (1860-1912); the latter's daughter Sophia Ann (1912-40) who married Frank Rhodes; and the Austrian former-Empress Zita (1940-49), a refugee from the war in Europe. In the 1950s, the house became a seniors' residence *La Villa Saint-Joseph*.

"Spencer Cottage"
1563 chemin St-Louis, Sillery.

Known as *Bagatelle*, this picturesque Italian-style villa was once home to the attaché of the Governor. Built near *Spencer Grange* by Henry Atkinson, also in 1849, it was famous for its miniature English garden which held indigenous and rare plants. A fire in 1927 destroyed the building which has been re-built according to the original plans. It is now owned by the City of Sillery and the house and gardens are open to the public. On display this summer, 2004, is an exhibition called "Times of the Tall Ships" which features photographs and recovered artifacts.

Outlying Communities of Quebec City

We visited eight communities with an English presence, encircling Quebec City on the shores of the St. Lawrence River, which bear witness to the diversified roles of English-speakers here.

First came settler-farmers, mostly from Ireland, after 1815. The great migration in the early 19th century resulted in over-crowding in Quebec City. The governor and the seigneurs (some English) planned settlements in the outer regions. Communities such as Shannon (Valcartier Station), Waterloo (Lake Beauport) and Ste-Agathe were first settled by English-speakers.

The quarantine station at Grosse Île was established in the 1830s to control the spread of cholera. Thousands of immigrants passed through this facility and many, mostly Irish, are buried here. The Celtic Cross and the remains of some buildings stand as monuments to this tragic chapter in our history.

English doctors played an important role in establishing the psychiatric hospital in Beauport, today called Centre Hospitalier Robert-Giffard.

English were prominent in the development of the power and forest resources of the Montmorency, Portneuf, Jacques Cartier and Chaudière Rivers. The lumber and pulp and paper industries were instrumental in the development of the communities of Chaudière Mills (Breakeyville), Portneuf, Pont Rouge and Donnacona. Some of the pioneers in these enterprises were the Fords, the Breakeys and the Bishops.

In the 1850s, English-speakers from the cities began to build summer houses in selected areas along the St. Lawrence River. In this region, we have the Dunns and Porteouses on Île d'Orléans, the Bignell family and others at Lake Beauport and salmon lodges such as the Jacques Cartier Salmon Club at Pont Rouge.

Today, most of the English have gone elsewhere, though some remain. The story of their contribution can be found in the place names (Shannon, Breakeyville), street names (chemin St. James Church, chemin Horatio Walker, Rang Armagh) and the remaining mills, houses and churches.

The Celtic Cross Memorial
Route 271, Ste. Agathe.

In 2003, the people of Ste-Agathe celebrated their 150th anniversary as a municipality. The few remaining English-speakers are the descendants of the Irish who arrived twenty to thirty years before 1853.

This memorial, erected in 2000 to commemorate over one hundred and fifty pioneer families, is dedicated "to the memory of our Irish ancestors and the brave journey that brought them to this land". This is inscribed in English, French and Irish. Among the names are O'Neill, Nugent, Hogan, Corrigan, Campbell and Wallace. Each family donated one hundred dollars to subsidize the cost of building the monument. Names on nearby farms today include Hogan, Kelly, Campbell and Murphy, indicating a continuing, but declining, English presence.

Immigrants often bring their differences to the New World. The Irish, though most were English-speaking, were both Protestant and Catholic. A story which illustrates the conflict is that of the Corrigan Affair as told by Lincoln Egan of Ste-Agathe. Corrigan, a Protestant, was judging animals in a competition. Some Catholics who disagreed with his decision gave him a beating, and Corrigan died. Later, another Corrigan killed an O'Donnell in reprisal. The atmosphere was so charged that some families moved elsewhere; for example, the Protestant Nugents moved to Kinnear's Mills. Pioneer life was a challenge in many ways.

The Maloney homestead

St. Peter's Range, Ste. Agathe.

Thomas Maloney came to Ste-Agathe from Waterford, Ireland in the mid-19th century. His farmhouse, now unused, dates from 1855. Pictured is Lincoln Egan, great-grandson of Thomas, who lived in this house with his family and worked the farm for many decades.

Ste-Agathe, and the surrounding towns of St. Giles, St. Sylvester and St. Patrick, are all villages which were developed mainly by Irish settlers. Lincoln Egan now lives in a residence in Ste-Agathe. He estimates the remaining English community at "about fifteen houses", mostly farmers. Relations with the French community are good, he says. The Sunday sermon is partly in French and partly in English and the St. Patrick's Day supper and dance draws a large attendance – two hundred and fourteen in 2004.

This property, no longer a farm, is now owned by Stephen Cameron, Lincoln's nephew, who lives here in a new house with his wife Diane. They have embarked on a project of re-forestation of this land.

The Hogan farmhouse

947 St. Michael's Range, Ste. Agathe.

The Hogans were among the first Irish families to settle in the Ste-Agathe area. Michael, the earliest arrival, received his lot in 1830. This is the Hogan farmhouse, built circa 1860 (the section on the left in the photo). It was originally faced with cedar shingles, still visible on the rear of the building.

Standing in front of the house is Eddy Hogan who owns and runs this dairy farm. His mother was French and Eddy considers himself to be both English and French. His children were raised in French, though two can also speak English. There is not much opportunity to speak English around here now, he says.

Eddy has a son who is keen to take over the farm, so the Hogan name will remain in Ste. Agathe.

St. Patrick's Church and cemetery
St. Patrick (St-Patrice-de-Beaurivage).

St. Patrick's was originally an Irish church when this area had a large Irish population. A local resident recalled a Father O'Reilly who served here. The statue of St. Patrick stands high on the front of the church in silent testimony to these former parishioners in this now predominantly French parish.

Both Irish and French are buried in the cemetery. Headstones remember people named Egan, Marquis, Horan, Demers, Burns, Bilodeau, Moran, Vachon and O'Reilly.

The Breakey groundwood mill
Rue St-Augustin, Breakeyville.

The Breakey family played a significant economic role along the Chaudière River for over one hundred years. Little remains of the Breakey mill today. Here, in the foreground, is the 1947 pump-house and behind it the groundwood mill – much changed. (A groundwood mill is a pulp mill where logs are turned into pulp and then shipped to other mills for the making of paper.)

The early Breakey mill, a pioneer on the Chaudière River, processed thirty-three million board feet of lumber per year into beams, planks, railway ties and telephone poles. Historian James E. Defebaugh described the Breakey mill in the early 1900s as, "one of the largest, if not the largest, spruce deal mill" in Quebec. For over a century, the Breakey lumber operations provided the chief economic activity along the Chaudière River. The Breakeys were entrepreneurial pioneers in the spirit of the Quebecois of the Beauce in the 20th century.

In 1960, the Breakeys sold their company to their nephew, Jack Scott, whose family ran the mill until the 1980s. It still operates today as Fibres Breakey (a division of Rolland and Cascades) and is one of North America's first plants to recycle by flotation, thus manufacturing pulp from re-cycled paper.

A Breakey house
Rue St-Augustin, Breakeyville.

Many impressive Breakey houses still stand here, along the river, just north of the mill. This Tudor-style house, built in 1904, and added to in 1912, was the home of Colin Breakey who became president of the company in 1930.

Pictured is Rex Scott, grandson of Ethel Breakey, sister of Colin. Jack Scott brought up his family, including his son Rex, in this house. Jack ran the ground-mill and the sawmills in the Beauce. Rex worked with his father and still owns timberlands in the Beauce, though he now works as an outfitter. He and his family are the last Breakey descendants living in Breakeyville.

Colin Breakey was the grandson of Hans Denaston Breakey who arrived in Lower Canada in 1830, at the age of twenty, from Rockcorrey, Ireland. The Irish Breakeys are descendants of French Huguenot emigrants to Ireland. Jean and Guillaume Bréquet started a linen bleaching business there circa 1700.

The decline of the business influenced young Hans Denaston to emigrate to Lower Canada. He first worked in a lumber-yard, then acquired his own. He formed a partnership with Charles King to erect a sawmill at what would become Chaudière Mills (and later, Breakeyville) and to acquire timberland in the Beauce. In 1847, the first timber drives were floated down the Chaudière River to their mill.

In the late 1870s, Hans' son, John, bought out the partners and became sole proprietor of four hundred and fifty-three square miles of timberland in Beauce County as well as the sawmill facilities at Chaudière Mills. In 1895, he employed six hundred men in the lumber camps in winter and two hundred at the mills and elsewhere in summer.

In 1908, John, who was Presbyterian, and his wife Helen Anderson, donated land and funds for the construction of a Catholic church in Chaudière Mills for the workers. In recognition, the parish was named Ste-Hélène and the municipality Ste-Hélène-de-Breakeyville.

When John Breakey died in 1911, management of the company passed to his widow Helen and his three sons, Andrew, Colin and John (Ian). Colin was educated at Cambridge and served in the French Ambulance Corps in World War I for which he received the Croix de Guerre. Under the management of the sons, the sawmill was transformed into a pulp mill. At the height of production, as many as two thousand men were employed during the timber drives.

Today, this house is an auberge, Manoir Breakey.

The Breakey Presbyterian Church
Rue de l'Eglise, Charny.

Charny, a railway centre, had a small English popula--tion with names such as Mountain and Woodward.

There is an unusual story attached to this church. Helen Breakey "received a fright" in the Breakeyville church and would no longer attend. "She was very Scottish," notes her descendant Alan Breakey. Helen's son, Andrew Denaston Breakey, built a replica of that church in Charny in 1920 in memory of his father, John Breakey. Anglicans shared this church, named St. Matthew's, with the Presbyterians. Anglican services ended in 1962.

It is now a private residence.

The Dr. Forrest house
150 rue Principale, Ste-Claire.

This 19th century house overlooks the Etchemin River in the village of Ste-Claire, once part of the seigneury of Louis Joliet. It was built in the late 1850s for Dr. William Wilson Forrest (1804-77) who came from a prominent Dublin family, (his father was secretary to the Earl of Selkirk in 1816-17). Dr. Forrest served in Bytown in the 1830s and was likely the first resident doctor in this area. Among his patients were the Henderson family, early developers of the region. Forrest married Clarissa Gethings, daughter of Capt. John Gethings of the 100 Newfoundland Regiment. Their daughter Julia Ann married Alexander the son of Gilbert Henderson. Dr. Forrest's great-grandson is Forrest Henderson, the last remaining Henderson in St. Malachy.

Dr. Maurice Lafontaine occupied the house in the 1940s and 1950s and it is now the home of Dr. Jacques Bechard who, when he had the windows of the house replaced, preserved the one where Dr. Forrest had etched his name on a windowpane. Dr. Forrest is buried in St. Paul's churchyard, St. Malachy.

The Dunn house

Chemin Bout de l'Île, Ste-Pétronille (Île d'Orléans).

Timothy Hibbard Dunn (1816-1898) was born in Maskinongé, Lower Canada, west of Three Rivers. His grandparents had come to Quebec from Vermont in 1778 as Loyalists. The family ran a mill, a blacksmith shop and a store. Timothy entered the timber trade in partnership with his brother, Charles, and Calvin & Cook Co. of Kingston. At this time, Britain ceased her preferential treatment for her colonies. T.H. Dunn was among a group of businessmen who joined an unsuccessful move towards annexation to the U.S. in 1849. In 1857, he took over the business as T. H. Dunn & Co.

Besides timber, Dunn was involved in pressing for a railway to Halifax, in industrial properties and manufacturing and was a principal supplier of oak to the Quebec market. His fortune was estimated at over one million dollars.

Timothy Dunn accumulated property at the south end of Île d'Orléans. With his son Logie and others, he assembled much of what would become the parish of Ste-Pétronille. He bought this family home, dated by the family as 1857 (and, perhaps, earlier), from a local businessman, and built an Anglican chapel and a three-hole golf course. Upon his death here in 1898, *The Montreal Star* observed that "Quebec loses one of her oldest and most prominent citizens, a self-made man of very large means, and one of the most patriotic of Quebeckers." Dunn descendants still live here.

St. Mary's Chapel
186 chemin Bout de l'Île, Ste-Pétronille (Île d'Orléans).

This Anglican chapel was built by the Dunns on their property in 1867 and is maintained by them to this day. Now surrounded by trees, it once stood in a field. Its size indicates the presence at one time of a considerable English summer population at Ste-Pétronille. Now, one service a year is held here.

The Dunn golf course
Ste-Pétronille (Île d'Orléans).

The three-hole Dunn golf course, next to St. Mary's, dating from the 1860s, is believed by some to be the oldest in North America. The story is told that each of the three sons of T. H. Dunn designed and constructed one hole on this private course.

Over the years, holes were added and now this is a private club used for the most part by French-speakers.

The Porteous residence

253 chemin Bout de l'Île, Ste-Pétronille (Île d'Orléans).

While most of the English and French who built summer homes outside Quebec City in the late 19th century and early 20th century did so west of the city, a few brave English souls found the beauty and isolation of Île d'Orléans to be worth the trouble and built their homes there. Île d'Orléans was then a mostly French agricultural island encircled by a road, rue Royale (not open in winter until 1948), which linked six small communities. Access was by boat until a bridge was built in 1935.

Among the first English to build here were the Porteous and Dunn families. Later arrivals included the Simons, Prices, Blairs and Holts.

The house, now owned by a religious order, is called Foyer de Charité Notre-Dame d'Orléans. Spirituality may have benefitted, but architectural integrity took a blow when an unharmonious chapel was added to the building.

Most of the English built in the Ste-Pétronille section of the island. Ronnie Blair, a long-time resident, underlines the existence of "first-class relations between French and English" here. English are less than one per cent of the population of the island today.

The Horatio Walker studio/house
Horatio Walker Street, Ste-Pétronille (Île d'Orléans).

What a splendid spot this is for a painter's studio, on the shore of "the Island", as it is referred to by its English inhabitants, gazing across the river to the Quebec City skyline and the spectacular Montmorency Falls. This house/studio, designed by architects Staveley & Staveley, was built in 1909 on Dunn land for Horatio Walker.

Walker, who is well-known for his paintings of rural life, was born in Listowel, Ontario, moved to New York and began to visit Ste-Pétronille in the summers. He became a permanent resident after 1900. His paintings can be found in many homes in the Quebec City area.

Grosse Île

This island in the St. Lawrence River below Quebec City served as a quarantine station from 1832 to 1937. The cholera epidemic of 1832 alerted the colonial authorities to the danger of importing disease to Lower Canada. The creation of this compulsory stopover for all passenger ships coming up the river helped to slow the spread of the great scourges of the time: cholera, typhus and smallpox. 1832 was a time of great distrust between the Canadiens, as French-Canadians were then called, and the ruling "Château Clique". Some of the former believed that the authorities imported disease to eliminate them.

English doctors played a prominent role in health care in the Quebec City region. Dr. James Douglas, co-founder of the Beauport Asylum, was president of the Board of Health in the city; and here on Grosse Île, his brother, Dr. George Mellis Douglas served from 1832 until 1864 – the most critical time in the spread of cholera and typhus – in various capacities, principally as medical superintendent.

The Celtic Cross

Standing forty-six feet tall on Telegraph Hill, one hundred and forty feet above the water, this monument made of grey Stanstead granite faces the river which brought so many to its shore. It was erected in 1909 to commemorate the thousands of Irish who ended their "sorrowful pilgrimage" here on Grosse Île. The inscriptions on the cross are in English, French and Irish (Gaelic); the Irish text is emotional and anti-British. The Ancient Order of Hibernians asked that every person of Irish descent in North America contribute one penny to help build this monument. Their work and contributions and the dedication of many in the late 20th century have helped to turn Grosse Île into a national memorial park both to the Irish buried here and to the doctors, priests and workers who risked, and in some cases, lost, their lives.

The famine graveyard

There are many cemeteries on this island. Unmarked crosses in the famine graveyard bear witness to those who were laid to rest in the trenches beneath. During the 1840s, "fever ships", riddled with typhus, brought the dead and the dying to the island in great numbers. 1847 saw the most burials on Grosse Île. In all, more than 6,000 people, mostly Irish, are buried here.

The Washhouse

In this building, immigrants went through a compulsory disinfection of their persons, their clothes and all their belongings – an agonizing experience. This 1855 building was used until a new operation was set up in 1893. After inspection and disinfection, immigrants went either to a hotel (classed according to the level of passage paid for) or a lazaret (hospital).

Grosse Île Hospital (Lazaret)

This is the oldest remaining building (1847) on the island and is the only one of the original twelve hospitals still standing. It was in these "lazarets" that the sick immigrants were treated. The lucky ones survived to face the difficult life of manual labour as factory workers, loggers, or as land pioneers; the unfortunate died and were buried on the island. The faint markings still preserved on the walls help us to realize the horrors these people experienced.

In the 1990s, Grosse Île became a national historic park administered by Parks Canada. It had been used as an animal quarantine facility by the Canadian government after 1937 and many buildings were torn down. This last remaining hospital was saved because it was used to house chickens. At last, the historic significance of Grosse Île has been recognized and the remaining buildings are being renovated and preserved.

Shannon

Twenty minutes by car north of Quebec City stands the community of Shannon, settled in the 1820s and '30s by pre-famine Irish seeking a better life. They became farmers and lumbermen, driving logs down the Jacques Cartier River (pronounced "Jackardy" by some here) to the mills at Donnacona.

The language of the Shannon Irish was English; the Irish language, having all but disappeared, was spoken by only a few of the arrivals. Today, about one-third of those living in the area speak English and almost all can trace their roots back to those immigrants of the 1820s and 1830s.

Shannon is one of Quebec's most strongly Irish rural communities. Elsewhere, in towns such as Sainte-Brigide-de-Laval, Donnacona, Frampton and St-Malachie, Irish roots have all but disappeared, submerged into the French-speaking mainstream. Streets crossing the Jacques Cartier River have names such as Wexford, Grogan and St. Patrick. The Irish have their own chapel, St. Joseph's, and a community centre with a capacity of four hundred. When the annual Shannon Irish Show is staged here, the hall is packed.

Place names familiar to many Shannon residents are evocative of Ireland: Kennedy's Hollow, McCloskey's Poplars, Brian Regan's Rock, Maher's Hill, Hickey's Hill, Murphy's Bridge, Paddy's Cut, Conway's Bridge and the thought-provoking Alley Broke Her Hip.

The Sunderland house
Ste. Catherine.

Built in the 1840s, this is the oldest house in the parish of Ste. Catherine. The late Eddy Conway, our guide, emphasized that the French and English-speaking Irish in the area live in harmony. Any confrontation, he insisted, is based on personal differences, not "race or language".

The Mulroney homestead
Ste. Catherine.

The Mulroneys came from Ireland and settled here in the early 1830s. In this modernized 19th century house, Benedict Mulroney, father of former Prime Minister Brian, was brought up. Mulroneys still live in the area, including Ena Mulroney Leahy who lives in this house. Mulroneys and O'Sheas are long-established families in the area of Ste. Catherine and Shannon. In his boyhood, Brian Mulroney spent summer days visiting his uncle, Jimmy O'Shea, a local turkey farmer.

The McCloskey barn
Shannon.

The McCloskey clan in Ireland were traditionally "retainers to the Chief". This 19th century barn, still in use, stands as a historic reminder of the Irish pioneers who opened up this land north of Quebec City.

The Stewart house
Wexford Road, Shannon.

Alexander Stewart, Scots-Irish from Donegal, built this log cabin circa 1880. Standing before it is the late Eddy Conway, an ex-mayor of Shannon and local historian. The Conways were original settlers in Shannon; their ancestral farmhouse, built one hundred and forty years earlier, was expropriated in the 1960s and the land was used to enlarge the Valcartier military training camp. Tears came to Eddy's eyes as he told how he was "treated like a criminal" by the agents who took his land and homestead away from him.

Valcartier offers an English education from kindergarten to grade 11 to its children and those of nearby Shannon, one reason why this English-speaking community survives. Shannon's future is still in doubt, however. An independent community since 1946 when it separated from the Parish of Ste. Catherine, it is now losing its young to jobs elsewhere. One hopes that with the intense Irish spirit which still thrives here, the Irish community in Shannon will not wither away as have so many others in Quebec.

75

The Robert Giffard Hospital
2601 chemin de la Canardière, Beauport.

After learning of innovations at the penal institute in Paris, Dr. Joseph Morrin came to believe that fresh air could be beneficial to the mind. In 1845, with three other doctors, Dr. James Douglas, Dr. Charles-Jacques Frement and Dr. Joseph Painchaud, he helped found Canada's first psychiatric hospital which was built on land that had been the seigneury of Robert Giffard in Beauport. It was called Asile de Beauport (or, the Quebec Lunatic Asylum). The first temporary asylum was in Giffard's old manor house.

Dr. Douglas, a ship's surgeon, had suffered a debilitating accident and turned from surgery to psychiatry. His son, also James Douglas, was one of the founders, in the 1880s, of the Douglas Hospital in Verdun.

Another hospital, Saint Michel Archange, was later built on this site. When it was destroyed by fire in the 1940s, this huge structure was built to replace it. The new Centre Hospitalier Robert-Giffard was named at a time when the Quebec government was seeking to reduce the number of saints' names in places and institutions.

Here is a fine example of an early Quebec institution built by both English and French.

The Bignell house
12 chemin de l'Ancêtre, Lake Beauport.

The Beauport seigneury was the oldest in Quebec. The first seigneur was Robert Giffard, the Marquis de Beauport, whose seigneury extended from Beauport on the St. Lawrence River twelve kilometres north-west to Lake Beauport. Most farmers on the seigneury worked land near the river, leaving the back country undeveloped.

In the early 19th century, Seigneur Antoine-Louis Duchesnay, who was also a member of the Legislative Assembly and the Executive Council, sought to develop the inland section of the seigneury. He divided it into six ranges which he offered for settlement to the increasing volume of British and Irish immigrants arriving after 1815.

The early arrivals on Waterloo Settlement – as it came to be known – were listed as farmers and "other trades". Two of the earliest were William Shadgett and John French – yeomen. Early families, arriving between 1823 and 1825, were those of Patrick Smith – surveyor; George Morrison – farmer; Lawrence Cribbon – mason; John Greer – labourer; and others.

In 1844, lumber baron Peter Patterson, who owned a mill at Montmorency Falls, became the ninth seignior. The Beauport-Waterloo Settlement, according to the 1851 census, was home to three hundred and ninety-one individuals, mostly Irish, two hundred and thirty-four of whom were born in Canada. In 1853, Waterloo Settlement became St. Dunstan-du-Lac Beauport. Now named Lac (Lake) Beauport, it celebrated its 150th anniversary in 2003.

This house was built circa 1848 and bought circa 1855 by William Bignell, a Quebec City notary, from a Dr. Morrison. It was used as a residence and later as a summer villa. It remained in the Bignell family until 1977.

St. James Church

Chemin St. James Church, Lake Beauport.

The Anglican parish here was founded in 1837 and this charming little church was built in 1890. The congregation is aging and declining and, as is so often the case in Quebec, finding it difficult to maintain the church. St. James is, however, still an active church with bi-monthly services. It is a popular spot for weddings.

Lake Beauport is a bedroom community for Quebec City and a resort and skiing area. The remaining English here are mostly cottage owners.

The Allsopp Manor
15 rue Notre Dame, Cap Santé (Jacques Cartier village).

George Allsopp's acquisition of the seigneuries of Cartier and d'Auteuil in 1773 signaled an important change in the local economy. He built a sawmill and a flour mill on the Jacques Cartier River and employed nearly two hundred men constructing mills, forest cutting and sawing commercial lumber. The boards were sent to Quebec City and Montreal. In the 1780s, Allsopp was one of the top flour producers in Quebec.

He came to Quebec from England in 1761 and married Ann Bondfield, daughter of a Quebec City merchant, with whom he had nine children. Allsopp was involved in government as General Commissioner of the Army and Defense in 1775, as a member of the Legislative Council and a judge of the Appeal Court.

He was a champion of the English merchants who in this era were battling the governors for political control in the colony. The merchants hoped to dominate politics and the economy at the expense of the Canadiens. Governor Haldimand dismissed Allsopp as a councillor in 1783, thus ending his political career.

Allsopp Manor dates from the later 18th century. It is a designated historic site which attests to the economic enterprise of its owner.

Donnacona Paper Company housing
129-135 rue St-Laurent, Donnacona.

The Donnacona Paper Co. built its staff houses on high land overlooking the St. Lawrence River and the paper plant. Rue St-Laurent was known as "Rue des Anglais" in this period.

There was a village here, Jacques Cartier, during the French régime. A Catholic church was built during the Seven Years' War and a fort – Fort Cartier. French troops withdrew here after the Battle of the Plains of Abraham. It was, in 1760, the last French stronghold taken by the British in the area.

The early developers of Donnacona were George Allsopp, the Sewells and John Foreman. The Donnacona Paper Co. was formed by a group of Americans to acquire and develop the timber resources and water power of the Jacques Cartier River region. George McKee, general manager, purchased the lands from John Foreman in 1912. Authorization came from the Quebec government in 1913, when construction of a dam and a plant began under the supervision of McKee. The company provided modern electric lighting, water-works and a sewage system for the houses in the new town.

When Lomer Gouin's provincial government prohibited the export of pulp to keep manufacturing jobs in Quebec, investors were motivated to build paper plants such as Donnacona. In 1916, there were two hundred men in the woods and two hundred and fifty at the plant. Many Irish from Shannon worked as loggers, bringing wood downriver to the dam at Donnacona. A small English community grew here of which few remain today.

Donnacona Paper Co. installed modern machinery in 1916. Two machines performed a series of processes: grinding and mixing; screening and washing; chemical treatment; pressing, drying and rolling into the finished product. Amazingly, the total output at this time was consumed by one newspaper, *The New York Times.* It took the pulp of one good-sized tree to produce one copy (96 pages in 1916) of *The New York Sunday Times.*

Portneuf

Our guide in Portneuf was Molly Herring Richard, now in her eighties, a recently retired sheep farmer. One of the blessings of these journeys we make has been the array of helpful and knowledgeable amateur guides who have taken us around their domains. Memorable among these was the indefatigable Molly who has a great love and knowledge of Portneuf and a pedal-to-the-metal driving style.

Christ Church
4300 Rang de la Chapelle, Portneuf.

This Anglican church was built in 1842 by local farmers, mostly Protestant Irish, to serve early settlers from the British Isles. British in design, with its crenellated tower, it stands next to the Halesboro cemetery where headstones bear such English names as Webb, Jess, Kingsborough and Burns. The church was financed by Edward Hale, uncle of Jeffrey Hale.

A service is held here once a year to pay homage to the men and women who helped develop the Edward Hale seigniory. Some members of the congregation are descendants of these pioneers. Pictured is Molly Richard who is active in preserving the church.

The Edward Hale manor house
100 First Avenue, Portneuf.

The first settler in the Portneuf area was Pierre Robineau in 1636. The seigneury of Portneuf was created in 1647 and in 1681 became a barony which included a flour mill, a sawmill, a church and a manor house. In 1801, a Mr. McNider took a fifty-year lease on the property which was taken over by Edward Hale, a member of the Council of Lower Canada. It is possible that he built this manor house which is now under restoration. Edward Hale was important in the early development of the Portneuf area, bringing in settlers, many of them Protestant Irish.

The Joe Ford paper mill
Portneuf

Joe Ford was a lad of eighteen when, in 1850, he decided to leave Glossip, England and work his passage as a sailor on a ship bound for Quebec. After six rough weeks at sea, on what turned out to be a condemned ship, he arrived. While walking on St. Paul Street, Joe passed a paper store owned by Angus McDonald, the founder of the paper industry in Portneuf. Joe had experience as a dyer in his father's mill and when he demonstrated this to Angus McDonald, he was given a job in the Portneuf mill. And, thus began the saga of the J. Ford & Company, eventually the dominant industry in the town.

During the French régime, the seigneurs gave precedence to settlement and agriculture. With the arrival of the English in the early 1800s more emphasis was placed on commercial exploitation of the forest and of hydraulic power. Industry began in Portneuf in 1806 when W.B. Coltman built a water-powered sawmill. Lumber mills, shipbuilding and, later, paper mills were developed by such men as Coltman, Angus McDonald, John Smith, Alexander Logan and, later, Joe Ford. The paper industry became the engine of the local economy: revenue, work, payrolls and spin-off into related industries, followed by the development of the community with its churches, schools and stores.

This was No. 2 mill which made felt paper. The J. Ford & Company produced varied paper products such as roofing paper, wallpaper, toilet paper, waxed paper and napkins.

"The Old Stone House"
Portneuf

On a hill overlooking the Ford mills stands this stone house (circa 1840), home, from 1841, of John Smith a paper-maker from Roslyn, Scotland. Soon after Joe Ford arrived to take up his job at the Portneuf mill, he became seriously ill. He was well cared-for in this house by Mrs. John Smith and her daughters, one of whom, Mary, he married two years later. He would one day live in this house.

Angus McDonald, son of Mrs. Smith by her first husband, was an exceptional entrepreneur who operated two paper mills, nail, saw, carding and flour mills and a general store. He was the seignior of Portneuf for a time, justice of the peace and owner of a small fleet of ships. In 1841, he built a mill which would later be the site of the No. 2 mill of the J. Ford & Co.

In 1857, McDonald lost everything when he invested in the North Shore Railway. His properties were sold to George Burns Symes, and Joe Ford lost his job. Joe kept working, rafting on the St. Lawrence River and eventually, with the help of Alexander Logan, he built a third mill on the Portneuf River where the No.1 mill of J. Ford & Co. stands today.

"Edale Place" *Portneuf*

Edale Place, named after the Ford home in England, was built in the late 1890s on land above the mills for Thomas Ford, son of Joe. A Ford descendant-by-marriage still lives here. The first English school in Portneuf was built on this property, but due to the declining English population here the children are now educated in Jacques Cartier Village.

Since 1886, the paper company was called J. Ford & Co. which included Joe's two sons, Joseph, Jr. and Thomas. In 1912, they bought out their father's share and were in partnership until 1930. Joseph, Sr. died in 1922 and Thomas in 1935.

French-speakers began operating mills in Portneuf in the second half of the 19th century. J.-Alphonse Lemay was one of these who showed vigour and initiative in his enterprise.

In the 1960s, the J. Ford & Company was one of only two independent family-owned paper companies left in Canada. This feat owed a great deal to the solid foundation laid by its 19th century founder. Later, it was still called the J. Ford Co., but it was no longer run by the Ford family. In 1995, the company was sold to Cédrico; it was closed in 2003 with a loss of one hundred and eighty jobs. An Ontario company has since shown an interest in buying the plant and re-activating some machines.

The Bishop and Sons paper mill
100 Bishop Road, Portneuf.

Thomas Parkin Bishop bought a mid-19th century nail factory from the Webb brothers in the late 1860s and turned it into a felt paper mill for the making of asphalt shingles. From right to left in the photo: the old nail factory, which became the rag-processing building; the two middle sections which were used for stock preparation; and the last building which was a de-fibrator. At its height, this mill employed close to two hundred people.

Thomas Bishop married Corinne Collette of St. Basile. Larry Thomson, a Bishop descendant, said, "If you didn't marry a French girl, you had to marry your cousin."

No longer a mill, this series of buildings is being re-modeled by Montreal decorator Peter Herring as a unique second residence – an architectural, engineering and decorating feat.

A Bishop house

120 Bishop Road, Portneuf.

There are a number of Bishop houses in Portneuf. This one, known as "the miller's house", is located next to the paper mill and the Portneuf River. It is believed to have been bought by T. P. Bishop from the Webb brothers about the same time as the mill.

A fire in 1977 destroyed part of the interior and the house stood unoccupied until the 1990s when it was bought and restored to its historic glory by René Lemieux, a Laval University professor who takes pride in the history of the house and emphasized how important the Bishops and the Fords were to the early development of Portneuf.

Woodend cemetery gate

Chemin Neuf, Portneuf.

Many of the English developers of Portneuf are buried here in Woodend Cemetery. This gate was donated by Glenn Ford, the actor, who appeared in such Hollywood movies as *Gilda*, *The Big Heat* and *Blackboard Jungle*. He is a member of the Portneuf Ford family, who was born in Quebec City but spent some of his early years here. He donated the gate in memory of RCAF Flying Officer Stewart Bishop (1916-1945) of Portneuf.

It is said that Glenn Ford wishes to be buried here.

The Toll Station

Chemin du Roi (King's Road), Pont Rouge.

The British built the Royal Bridge – known locally as Dery's bridge – and the toll station in 1801. It was at that time the only bridge traversing the Jacques Cartier River, and the British levied tolls for crossing. A notice posted on the toll house reads, in part:
Tolls:

1 cart (2 wheels) with a horse .... .05c.

A horse or mare .... .025c.

Beef or cow .... .02c.

A walker, by each day .... .01c.

"Every person who will pass on the bridge with carts, horses, beefs, or cows must pay in going and coming back but only once a day and the same rate will be required either in summer or in winter. People making pass too much heavy load will be responsible of the damages made to this bridge."

Local people who objected to the tolls built their own bridge and painted it red, giving the village its name – Pont Rouge. The house is known as the Déry house, after a later occupant. It was used for a time by the Donnacona Paper Co. as temporary housing for English staff and is now a tourist information centre.

The Jacques Cartier salmon lodge

71 rue Pleau, Pont Rouge.

Salmon-fishing on the Jacques Cartier River was described as early as 1839. It was a favourite pastime of British officers and the affluent English of this area in the 19th century. The last owner of this lodge, which stands near the river, was Andrew Paton who was married to Margaret Boswell of the Quebec City brewing family. A "the-horse-knows-the-way" story is told of Andrew Paton, who, "a bit the worse for wear" one night, arrived home in his sleigh delivered by the horse.

Construction of dams and the industrial use of the river's water resulted in the disappearance of the salmon from the Jacques Cartier River. Today, authorities are attempting to revive the salmon run by building cement steps to encourage the salmon to once again make their ancient journey up this river.

The St. Maurice

The English dominated the exploitation of the natural resources of the St. Maurice region from the middle of the 19th century to the middle of the 20th century. Why? The answer can be found in education and access to capital.

The Scots and English valued an education that included science, commerce and engineering, at basic and advanced levels. French education, on the other hand, was controlled by the Catholic Church which frowned on commercial activity. The brightest French students became doctors, lawyers, teachers and priests. And, so, industrial development was left to the English.

While French-speaking entrepreneurs struggled to obtain capital, the English had easy access to the most advanced industrialized nations in the world, Great Britain and the United States of America. And, the Quebec government encouraged such foreign investment. Thus, it was English-speaking investors and engineers who built the dams, power plants, pulp & paper mills, aluminum smelters and chemical plants that flourished from Three Rivers to La Tuque on the St. Maurice River which runs through the heart of Quebec. The owners and bosses were English and the available cheap labour was primarily French. Local Shawinigan historian Jean Harnois told us that in the early 1940s there were only four French-speaking civil engineers in all of Quebec.

The Quiet Revolution of the 1960s would change the balance. Hydro power was nationalized and the education system was overhauled so that young French graduates could compete in the world of industry and commerce. Today, most of the management and skilled workers in the St. Maurice are French. The English have all but disappeared from this region, but they have left an important legacy.

Three Rivers

Three Rivers was first fortified by the French in 1634. In addition to its role in defense, this site was important in the fur trade and as a missionary centre. Many of Canada's greatest explorers lived here: Nicolet, Radisson, des Groseilliers and de la Vérendrye.

The economy of the region was based first on the fur trade. In 1733 the St. Maurice ironworks were opened. Economic development was slow until the middle of the 19th century with the building of Canadian and American lumber mills. By the turn of the 20th century Three Rivers would become one of the main centres of newsprint production, sending its product to such cities as New York, Boston and Chicago.

Saint James Anglican Church

181 rue des Ursulines, Three Rivers.

The first building on this site was a wooden Recollet monastery built in 1693 and replaced by this stone structure in 1754. The British took it over in 1760, but did allow the monks to live out their lives here. In the meantime, it was used as a garrison chapel (from 1761), a court house, a storehouse for medicines and supplies, a military hospital, a jail and sheriffs' offices.

By 1777, the buildings came under Anglican ownership. The first Protestant service was held in 1768, with a Swiss minister. Bishop George Mountain tried to set up a theological college here in 1840, but with the founding of Bishop's College at Lennoxville in the 1840s, the project was dropped.

As is the case for many Christian congregations in the province, both English and French, a diminishing attendance has created problems for St. James. In a pamphlet history of the church is this handwritten notation, "1999 financial difficulties. Small group struggling". A Quebec City minister leads a service once a month and local wardens provide a weekly service. Attendance is said to range between four and twenty-two. Other congregations such as the Pentecostal and the Dutch Reform use the premises, which helps with expenses.

The Ezekiel Hart monument

Champlain Park, Hart Street, Three Rivers.

The Hart family were prominent citizens of Three Rivers in the 18th and early 19th centuries. Aaron Hart, a commissary officer in the British army during the Seven Years' War, settled here after 1760. He became a seignior, and records indicate that he was a popular leader. He was also a successful businessman who founded a family which played a prominent role in commerce, literature and sports. (A coach of the Montreal Canadiens in the 1920s and '30s was a descendant, Cecil Hart. The NHL Hart trophy was donated by Richard Hart, Cecil's father.)

Ezekiel Hart, son of Aaron, a Three Rivers merchant, was the first Jew ever elected to an Assembly in the

British Empire. He was elected in 1807 and again in 1808 to the Legislative Assembly, but was declared ineligible both times because he was a Jew. He was nominated again in 1809, an indication of the respect in which he was held in Three Rivers, but he decided to withdraw. Not until 1832 did Jews gain the right to represent their communities in the Legislative Assembly.

The small but vibrant Jewish community in Three Rivers has disappeared. The synagogue on rue des Forges no longer exists and the remains from the cemetery were disinterred and buried in Mount Royal Cemetery in Montreal. This monument on Hart Street, in a prominent place in the old city, is testimony to the role played by the Hart family in Three Rivers and to the respect in which they are held by its people.

The William Ritchie house
693 rue Des Ursulines, Three Rivers.

This painted brick house, built in stages beginning in 1893, stands on historic rue des Ursulines, in old Three Rivers, beside the St. Lawrence River.

Three generations of the Ritchie family lived here. William Ritchie, one of many English entrepreneurs in the region, opened a sawmill in 1896 on l'Île St-Christophe in the delta of the St. Maurice River.

The Wayagamack pulp and paper mill
Île de la Potherie, Three Rivers.

In 1910, industrialist Charles R. Whitehead founded the Wayagamack mill on the second island at the mouth of the St. Maurice River. This mill produced newsprint, kraft paper and paperboard. Whitehead's textile mill, Wabasso (1908) and Wayagamack played an important role in the modernization of Three Rivers. This mill is now owned by Kruger and is called Kruger-Wayagamack.

Company row houses

785-819 rue St-Paul,
Three Rivers.

Managers, master electricians, engineers, foremen and other English skilled labour lived in these row houses.

The town was under British administration after 1760. Scots and English were the first English-speakers to settle here. They held jobs in management and as engineers and skilled labour. Unskilled Irish labour came later.

Whitehead house

858 Terrasse Turcotte,
Three Rivers.

Built in 1850 by then-mayor of Three Rivers J.-E. Turcotte, this house is known to English-speakers as the Whitehead house. This handsome residence which faces the harbour in old Three Rivers was later home to important local industrialists Alexander Baptist and Charles R. Whitehead.

When Wabasso closed in the 1980s, the plant was demolished. Its disappearance alerted many local citizens to the loss of their heritage and sparked the preservation of old Three Rivers.

The former Three Rivers High School and the Anglican cemetery
St. François-Xavier and De Tonnancour, Three Rivers.

There have been English schools in Three Rivers since the 1760s, created first to educate the children of British soldiers and merchants. Records show that there was a Protestant academy as early as 1857. This school, built in 1919, had become overcrowded by 1940 thanks to the population growth resulting from industrial expansion. It is now being used by the provincial government as an administrative centre.

The school stands behind one of the oldest English cemeteries in Quebec. The headstones, some dating back to its founding in 1808, are often difficult to decipher. It is believed that one of General Wolfe's officers, a Lieut. Sinclair, is buried here. Bell and Ritchie are among the prominent Three Rivers names inscribed on the headstones.

The cornerstone of the new high school at 1241 rue Nicolas Perrot was laid in 1946 by then-Premier Maurice Duplessis. Shortly after this, the English St. Patrick's School was built nearby. Today, Three Rivers High School educates both elementary and secondary students and demonstrates a phenomenon that exists throughout the cities of Quebec which once had substantial English populations. According to the present English-speaking principal Bill Dousett (he believes his surname is Jersey English), the school's student body is about 15% English, 5% French using the grandfather clause, and the remainder the children of French/English mixed marriages. Some are French Protestants. Approximately 50% of the school's graduates go on to the local French CEGEP, while the remainder who continue their education go to English CEGEPs in Quebec City, Lennoxville and Montreal.

The St. Maurice forges

Chemin des Forges, Three Rivers.

Canada's first iron foundry was opened in 1733 during the French régime. It is certainly a French landmark, but the English played an important role here for almost one hundred years, running the forges from 1787. Matthew Bell was the sole administrator for over half a century (1793-1846) and is recognized today by French historians as a man who "made a definite mark in the history of the St. Maurice Forges". (R. Boissonault) Pictured is the last remaining foundry, over-looking the St. Maurice River. The last owners of the forges were the McDougall family, from 1863 to 1883 when the forges were extinguished for the last time due to a difficult economic climate. The vast grounds of this site are beautifully cared for with walkways, picnic sites and information centres, recollecting an industry started by the French and continued by the English.

Shawinigan

On a visit to Shawinigan in 1913, Beckles Willson described the St. Maurice River: "Some four and twenty miles up the St. Maurice the river is narrowed by two rocky projections and an island which divides its deep channel in twain. Then comes the drop in level and a swift rush of foaming waters, fall after fall, leap after leap, the whole mighty flood dashes down, hurling itself against barriers of adamant.... Such are the Shawenegan [*sic*] Falls...."

Here, English entrepreneurs harnessed the hydraulic power of the St. Maurice River and developed industries: Shawinigan Water & Power; Alcoa (Aluminum Company of America) and its subsidiary Alcan (Aluminum Company of Canada); Belgo (pulp and paper); and Canadian Industries Limited (electro-chemistry), which would bring great change to the region. By the 1940s, Shawinigan Falls would be one of Canada's most prosperous cities.

The Shawinigan Falls dam

There are two dams at this juncture on the St. Maurice River including this, the original Shawinigan Water & Power dam, built (circa 1900) at the beginning of the modern industrialization of Quebec. Logs from as far up the St. Maurice River as La Tuque were once floated through Grand'mere and Shawinigan Falls to Three Rivers. The logs had a company mark and were sorted at each mill site – "ours", "yours". "Yours" were sent on to the next mill.

The floats are a thing of the past, since the logs are now trucked. And the powerful falls as described by Beckles Willson in 1913 have all but disappeared, tamed by man and industry.

The Shawinigan Water & Power plant

This company built the foundation upon which Quebec was industrialized in the first half of the 20th century, whereby the province began its transformation from the dominance of agriculture to that of industry. When Shawinigan Water & Power was formed in 1898, electricity was in its infancy. The company, a pioneer in electrical engineering and financed primarily by British and American capital, became the world's second-largest hydro-electric centre – after Niagara – feeding the public and corporate need for electricity.

The St. Maurice River, in addition to its great source of water power, was an area rich in forest resources and cheap labour. Big families and poor farmland generated a ready work-force. The company encouraged customers to become shareholders in the company. By 1932, Canadians owned seventy-two per cent of company shares.

Water power was under the control of the provincial government which had a policy of selling this resource (on the assurance of proper utilization). Between 1900 and 1910, power production in Quebec increased by three hundred and ten per cent. By 1914, three companies monopolized the industry: Shawinigan Water & Power, Montreal Light, Heat & Power and Southern Canada Power (Eastern Townships).

The original power-house (1901), which stood on the left of the photo, no longer exists. This is power-house Number 2 (1911). In 1928, the company received an eighty-five year lease from the Quebec government covering all the power of the rapids of the St. Maurice River from above La Tuque to La Gabelle (at the forges). By 1932, this company supplied both public and corporate power to Montreal, the St. Maurice region, Charlevoix, the Eastern Townships, the Lower St. Lawrence and Quebec City.

In 1963, the Quebec Liberal government under the leadership of Premier Jean Lesage and his Resources Minister, René Lévesque, declared the lease void and nationalized the industry. Ownership reverted to the province. This was a controversial issue. Ontario had controlled its own hydro-power since the 1930s, but in Quebec, English entrepreneurs and research had built and developed the industry and owned it. Though they had operated under strict government regulations, having to build unprofitable power lines to some regions, they could nevertheless give preferential treatment to important industrial consumers and also export power for profit, thereby discouraging consumption by small Quebec industries, farms and residences. They and their shareholders were loath to relinquish this prerogative.

Now, Quebecers rely on a government corporation responsible to the people, rather than a private company answering to its shareholders, to provide hydro-electric power to the province. In reflecting upon this issue, we must remember that it was English entrepreneurs and engineers who first built Quebec's vast hydro system. It was they who tackled the wilderness and risked capital to develop this resource.

By 1963, one hundred and ninety of the two hundred and forty-three engineers at Hydro-Quebec were francophones. The Quiet Revolution would result in the training of more French engineers who would help to build the great dams on the Manicouagan River and at James Bay. The motto "Maître Chez Nous" was set in motion.

The Alcan smelter
Shawinigan.

John Joyce, a businessman from Boston, visited here in the 1890s and acquired the rights to the falls from the Quebec government. The first industry to be developed was Shawinigan Water & Power in 1898 (on the right is their building erected in 1911). In 1899 Northern Aluminum Company, a subsidiary of Alcoa, became the first customer of Shawinigan Water & Power when they built Canada's first aluminum plant (on the left) which began producing primary aluminum in 1901; at the top of the photo is the second Alcoa plant.

In 1928, Northern Aluminum Co. became The Aluminum Company of Canada (Alcan), independent of Alcoa. This company spread throughout Canada, from the Saguenay to Kitimat, B.C., and developed into an international company. It was here in Shawinigan that it got its start. Today, this historic building is part of la Cité de l'Energie, a combination science centre and museum.

An Alcan manager's house
1415 Maple Street, Shawinigan.

Corporations were obliged to build entire towns in the wilderness to house and serve the company staff and workers. In 1899, Shawinigan Water & Power Company engaged the Montreal engineering firm Pringle and Son to design a plan for a town to serve the industries developing at Shawinigan. The Boston landscaping company of the Olmstead brothers visited and made suggestions which are evident in the abundance of greenery and the way the roads give access to vistas. The architects hoped that the design, inspired by the Garden City Movement in England, would "create harmony".

The town's English minority was housed on the more attractive sites on riverbanks and hills, away from the fumes of industry. This is the last of the Alcan managers' houses (built by the company) still used by Alcan. It stands on Maple Street, known as "rue des bosses" to many French who lived in tenements closer to the river. It can be said that these industrial towns were designed to ensure profits, relying on social control to guarantee rule by the business elite. The company towns fueled nationalist feelings which would lead to the Quiet Revolution.

The Catholic Church, unlike the government, was opposed to industrial development and demanded that the English owners make a deal with the local bishop. Land had to given for a parish church, largely paid for by the company, and control over the social life of the workers was put in the hands of the parish priest.

The George Street houses

George Street, Shawinigan.

In 1916, Shawinigan Water & Power undertook the task of building houses for their mid-level workers, the majority of whom were English. Montreal architect David J. Spence was brought in to design the project of English-style row houses. Forty-four houses built in groups of two, three or five units with landscaping and trees went up on Connaught (later, George) Street. The rents were only $14-$18/month and the company took care of all maintenance. The residents put hearts over their doors and the area was nicknamed "street of hearts". The houses are still there, though quite changed. Some hearts still remain.

Shawinigan High School

Today, the English Protestants of Shawinigan attend St. Stephen's Church in Grand'mere (if they can get transport. Many are aged) and the students from Grand'mere go to Shawinigan High School. A sign of the diminishing English population here, the student body now includes many children of mixed marriages and French children eligible under the grandfather clause. The size of this 1926 building attests to the prominence of the English here in the mid-20th century.

Dorothy Munro Jomini, our helpful and informative guide, who attended this school in the 1920s and '30s, extolled the fine teaching here "by farmers' daughters from the Eastern Townships" and told of a French Catholic boy who had demanded to attend the high school because of the "wonderful education". The declining numbers of English here now, and the rise of the French to the management level, has reduced tension between the two language groups. Another of our guides, Jean Harnois, said that many French, including himself, are ready to view the English past with more openness and interest.

Grand'mere

Grand'mere was a true company town. The Laurentide Pulp and Paper Company was the largest employer and undertook to create a planned community where it: built houses for the management, skilled staff and workers; created a park, a company golf course and a curling club; erected a hospital, a hotel and an assembly hall for recreation; ran a farm which provided dairy products, meat and vegetables for the community; gave land for the church; and even set up an air service which was a pioneer in commercial aviation in the 1920s.

George Chahoon (1872-1951), an American from Ithaca, NY, became president of Laurentide in 1902 and served the company for nearly thirty years. It was he who was responsible for providing many of these services. When consolidation took place in 1930, Chahoon was forced out.

The Grandmother rock
Rock Park, 6th Avenue, Grand'mere.

Nature created her; the aboriginals spun legends around her; the French christened her; and the English removed her from the St. Maurice River and reconstructed her in the middle of the town which bears her name. The rock, with a profile resembling that of an old woman, which had for eons occupied its place in the falls of the river, stood in the spot where the Laurentide Company wanted to build a power plant. Hesitating to destroy the rock, the company paid $13,000 to have it dynamited and rebuilt away from the river. The story is told that every piece was numbered so that the rock could be reassembled as it had been. Unfortunately, the man in charge died before the reconstruction and we are left to wonder if grandmother is exactly as she was. In any case, the rock has been rebuilt with a recognizable profile of an old woman and presides with dignity over present-day Grand'mere. And, the power plant was erected where she once stood.

The Laurentide Pulp and Paper power plant
St. Maurice River, Grand'mere.

A French hamlet of a few houses grew here before the advent of the pulp and paper companies. In 1880, industrialist John Foreman was the first to attempt to link the hydraulic power of the river with the resources of the forest. A sawmill and a pulp mill were developed on the right bank of the St. Maurice and the beginnings of Grand'mere emerged. In 1887, the Laurentide Pulp Company built a mill here using oxen for its construction. For the next ten years, only pulp was produced here. The capital came from Canadian, American and British entrepreneurs; the management and skilled staff were English-speaking, many of them American; the work force was almost entirely French. In 1897, construction began on the paper and sulphite mill and by 1899 there were three digesters and three paper machines in operation. Modern industry had come to Grand'mere.

The need for electric power had been anticipated from 1900. A power plant (seen here) was completed in 1915. The plant was designed on the fortress-like lines of the cathedral of Ste. Cécile in Aldi, France. The finely wrought brickwork in the arches and piers surrounding the windows display a craftsmanship rarely found today. Now, this is part of the Hydro-Québec network. The dominance of Laurentide, Canada's first manufacturer of newsprint in the early 1900s, gave way to other companies: Bathurst, Stone and, today, Abitibi- Consolidated. Local English people, however, remember Laurentide as the creator of modern Grand'mere.

The Laurentide time office, *Grand'mere.*

This building constructed from dark-stained peeled logs, and with a steep Viking-style roof, is believed to have been part of the original mill complex. Once the punch-in time office, it is now the entry guard post and houses the offices of the co-op for employees' savings.

The Laurentide Inn
10 – 6th Avenue, Grand'mere.

The large central section of this hotel is the original wood-frame structure, with fine interior paneling and beamed ceilings, built by the Laurentide Company in 1897. Its purpose was to attract businessmen to Grand'mere and to provide board and lodging for Laurentide staff and guests. A 1913 visitor described "everything neat and comfortable...a bathroom adjoining, with hot and cold water...and from my window..flowerbeds and lawns and creeper-clad cottages."

The Inn was once furnished with antique furniture from the Menier chateau on Anticosti. Paul Desmarais leased the Inn for ten years and when he left he took the Menier furniture with him. In recent years, the old inn, with additions, has operated as the Auberge Grand'mere. It has been the subject of controversy, with its involvement in the "Shawinigate" affair and a recent fire. The local English still call it "the Inn".

The Assembly Hall
opposite Auberge Grand'mere, Grand'mere.

This handsome stone building, designed in a romantic style with a turret reminiscent of Normandy, was put up by the Laurentide Company under the presidency of George Chahoon to provide the downtown (mainly English) people of Grand'mere with a meeting place. Among the activities held here were: meetings, social gatherings, parties, school activities, stage plays, ballroom dances, badminton, basketball and wedding receptions. Later, an addition was made which housed a men's club for managers and other company officials. It had paneled walls and billiard tables and a requirement for membership of the then-handsome annual salary of $5,000. One can imagine air that was blue with cigar smoke.

In the early days, the French had their own community centres in the upper town. French members began joining this club in the 1940s. The Assembly Hall and the Park were given to the city and, today, this is a cultural centre, La Maison de la Culture.

St. Stephen's Anglican Church

4th Avenue at 1st Street, Grand'mere.

The first Anglican church in Grand'mere, "a small and crude structure", was built in 1899. In 1900, records tell us, there were fifty "souls" and forty-four services. By 1920, there were four hundred and thirty-nine in the congregation and sixty-four services and a second church, somewhat higher up the hill, had replaced the first.

The third church (photo), erected in 1924, moved the congregation still higher up the hill. This sturdy stone church with its slate roof and hand-carved Casavant organ was built for an affluent and educated population.

Today, there are an estimated fifty English-speakers remaining in Grand'mere. Even with the addition of those from Shawinigan, the church services average a congregation of between eight and fifteen. A minister is supplied by the Diocese of Quebec for Communion services once a month. A francophone former Catholic priest has been accepted by the Diocese and is forming a French congregation whose numbers are increasing. A candlelight service on the Sunday before Christmas is well-attended and popular with the local French people.

First and second row houses
Place Consol, Grand'mere.

The Laurentide Company laid out the roads and built the houses for its employees. 1st and 2nd Avenue houses were assigned to English staff of the mill. Upper management were given the more substantial houses on 3rd Avenue and above, but the Superintendent lived on 1st Avenue to be close-by for any problems arising at the mill. These small but attractive first and second row houses were moved from their original sites to the newly created Place Consol to make room for needed parking close to the mill.

The Park and third row houses
3rd Avenue, Grand'mere.

"The Company encourages...all sports: free tennis courts, free bowls, free boating, free gymnasiums, free library, free billiards. Under such circumstances is it any wonder that Grandmother is popular? As one of the directors said to me, It sounds like philanthropy, but it is really first rate economics." (Beckles Willson)

Grand'mere was a town designed around a park. The Company created the park and planted the trees. They built tennis courts and a bandstand and laid out bowling greens. This is where the English gathered to play and to celebrate with band concerts and fireworks displays. Above and over-looking the park were the managers' houses.

Today, only two of the twenty houses are occupied by English people. The park, referred to with a residual resentment by some as "parc des Anglais", is well-cared for, the great trees still stand, but the bandstand and the tennis courts and the bowling green are gone.

The mill manager's house
90 Riverside Road, Grand'mere.

This too is a company house, built on higher ground over-looking the St. Maurice River, as were many of the homes of the company executives. Our guide Dorothy Jomini was born in Shawinigan and lived for over fifty years in Grand'mere. Though legally blind, Dorothy directed us unerringly through the twists and turns of this wooded area (all over the city, in fact) pointing out the significant sites.

The private Laurentide Golf Club was a company facility, created in 1910, with a club house built in 1920. This was one of the perks for company employees, offering special rates and preferential opportunities for summer employment for employees' children. This club is now owned by former Montreal Canadiens player Bobby Rousseau; the language most often heard on the links is French.

Many of the estates on Riverside Road were built by Chahoon, including his own which, sad to say, was demolished by his daughter upon his death. Other houses of his which remain are those built for his secretary, his golf pro, his gardener, and a nine-car garage which has been remodeled as a residence. Most of these houses are now owned by francophones.

The Laurentide Company farm
Route 153, Grand'mere.

In 1919, the company created this farm to provide clean milk and produce for its employees following the post-World War I influenza epidemic. It was built across the river from the town and, before the construction of a bridge (1929), the farm used scows to transport its goods.

The farm ended production in the 1940s and the land was sub-divided for housing. Some buildings were preserved and are now used by businesses or for storage. A silo, still visible at a distance, is a reminder of this part of Grand'mere's history.

Our guide was Chandler Williams who came here as a child and worked half his adult life in Grand'mere and half in Shawinigan at the paper mills. He was about to move (2003) to a residence in Shawinigan built on the site of the Cascade Inn, a Shawinigan Falls landmark destroyed by fire.

La Tuque

The Brown pulp mill
Chemin de l'Usine, La Tuque.

The forests and water power of the St. Maurice attracted the Brown Corporation of Berlin, New Hampshire to this area in the early 1900s. Before Brown, there was only a fur-trading post on the west side of the river. A town grew around the new mill and the railway came to La Tuque in 1908. In 1910, the mill produced fourteen tons of pulp.

The management of the company and skilled workers were English, and Brown also brought in Scandinavians who were in the forefront of the forest industries at the turn of the century. Wilhelm Loken and Odin Olsen, descendants of those early arrivals, worked for Brown and, now retired, have remained in LaTuque. They remarked that the young, both French and English, are leaving the town.

The La Tuque mill made only pulp which was transported to New Hampshire to be made into paper. The Brown Corporation operated until the 1950s when it was taken over by Canadian International Paper. It is now owned by Smurfit-Stone. In the 1960s, the company employed 1,600 workers; today, between five and six-hundred. The plant processes sawdust (75%) and chips into pulp. The smell of this industry permeates the air of La Tuque. This is the trade-off for what is the engine of the town. "If the plant closed," said Wilhelm Loken "the town would have nothing."

The Brown log house
Beckler Street, La Tuque.

This house, over-looking the St. Maurice River, stands at the end of Beckler Street which is lined with English-style houses. These were built by the company in the early 20th century for the use of its upper management who were mostly English. The log house, the largest and most impressive, was for the use of the mill manager. It was still the mill manager's house when, in June 2004 on the day after this photograph was taken, it suffered a devastating fire. Fortunately, there were no injuries but this historic landmark and its valuable contents, furniture, tapestries and paintings, were a total loss.

St. Andrew's Anglican Church
Beckler Street, La Tuque.

The Brown Corporation donated the land and built this church circa 1912. The resident minister's house stands in the background. There was no Lutheran church in La Tuque, so the Scandinavian Lutheran population joined the Anglican church.

As has happened with so many English-built communities on the Canadian Shield, the English population has diminished drastically, with La Tuque's now standing at about one per cent. An itinerant minister from Quebec City serves the remaining congregation.

La Tuque High School, which stands behind the church, once profited from the tendency of immigrants to educate their children in English. It now has a student body of about one hundred and fifty, only twenty per cent of whom are English. However, local people make a point of citing the friendly atmosphere which exists between the language groups in La Tuque.

The Brown community club
Beckler Street, La Tuque.

The Brown Corporation, like so many other companies in remote areas, built facilities to attract investment, professionals and skilled workers to its site. Brown built this centre for its employees in the 1920s. It is now home to the Knights of Columbus and is one of the few large halls in La Tuque.

The Beckler Street houses, *La Tuque.*

These English-style houses were built by the Brown Corporation for its upper management at the beginning of the 20th century. The street, originally known as On the Bank Street (and referred to by francophones, as were such streets in other towns, as "Rue des Anglais"), was later named in honour of Warren Beckler a long-time manager of the Brown Corp. and of Canadian International Paper (1945-60). The houses are now owned by Smurfit-Stone.

The Anglican residential school

Brown Street, La Tuque.

Beginning in the late 19th century, Christian churches in Canada, both Protestant and Catholic, created residential schools for native children. Their purpose, which later came into great disrepute, was to assimilate these children into the mainstream culture, particularly as to religion. The children were removed from their families and brought to the schools where they were forbidden to use their own language or practice the ways of their people.

This Anglican church and school were built in the 1960s to re-educate native children from around Quebec, many of them Montagnais. The criticism of this practice which first arose in the 1970s forced many of the schools to close, including this one. The buildings now stand idle, with broken and boarded up windows, an apt symbol of the damage caused by this misguided enterprise.

The Beauce

Today, the population of the Beauce is almost entirely French-speaking, but this was not always the case. In the early 19th century, British and Irish pioneers settled pockets of the region and, later, Jewish peddlers trekked up the Chaudière River with their wares as far as St-Georges.

Of the waves of Irish and British who came to Quebec after 1815, fleeing famine and poverty, most continued west, but many stayed in Quebec City. This threatened over-population, compelling the government to open up new townships to the north and the south of the city. Irish Protestants and Catholics and some Scots opened up new land along the Chaudière and Etchemin Rivers, creating the communities of Frampton, St. Malachy, Cumberland Mills and Jersey Mills.

Three landed proprietors, Edouard Desbarats (an assistant clerk in the Lower Canada Parliament) and William and Gilbert Henderson, were placed in charge of settlement. Desbarats, the founder of Frampton (named St. Edouard-de-Frampton in 1825, in his honour), had difficulty attracting French settlers from their seigneuries and so chose Irish immigrants, whom he considered "a hard-working people, sound of both mind and body and of a peaceful nature". The township of Frampton was established in 1806 and that year Desbarats acquired land in West Frampton. The Hendersons developed the area along the Etchemin River where St. Malachie (the Irish saint is now French!) stands today.

Settlers began moving into these areas after 1815 when rough roads had been built and early mills erected. The splendid countryside with vistas of high ridges and wide valleys, a palette of colour in the autumn, belied the rocky, almost barren soil beneath. Farming was exceedingly difficult and many men had to seek other jobs to support their families: lumbering, maple sugar production and mill work. As the English began to move on to better land in the Eastern Townships and the west, or to get jobs in Montreal, French settlers began to move into the Frampton area, particularly after the end of the seigneurial system in 1854.

The number of English families in Frampton Township peaked in 1865 at thirty-nine; in 1900, there were thirty-two. Frampton was incorporated in 1858 and a tradition was established to include the three founding peoples, Irish Catholics, Anglicans and French, on the town council. The Anglican seat was held until 1941.

English-speaking people also helped to open the upper Beauce, as we can see from the names on the headstones in the cemeteries at Cumberland Mills and Jersey Mills. Among the families who helped to build this region are the Breakeys who exploited the lumber resources and the Pozers who developed the seigniory where St-Georges-de-Beauce stands today.

Christ Church – "Springbrook"
Route 216, West Frampton.

Springbrook, built in 1837, is the oldest place of worship on the original missionary circuit of Frampton, Saint Malachy, Standon and Cranbourne. It began as a neo-Gothic fieldstone structure, later covered in stucco. The wooden bell tower, erected by local volunteers, was added in 1896. The church and cemetery stand on a hill away from the main road, reached by a wooded pathway. More than eighty headstones, with names such as Ross, Hurley, Hodgson and Bartholomew, still stand in the adjoining cemetery. Married women from some pioneer families are interred next to their kin, while their husbands are buried elsewhere in the cemetery.

Some of the pastors here were educated at Bishop's College in Lennoxville. One of these was Gerald F. Hibbard who served from 1898 to 1942. In 1898, his wife, Elfrida Musgrove Calcutt, originated the idea of the "Anglican quilt". Members of the congregation would pay to have their signatures sewn onto the quilt – a fund-raiser for the Hibbard's private school. The 1917 quilt has three hundred and seventy-seven names. With a diminishing Protestant population, the *Springbrook* mission became inactive in 1947. When the last Anglican families left the area in 1952, the forget-me-nots, previously planted, began to flourish at the church site.

Untended, the church began to deteriorate. It was saved by a francophone organization formed in 1984 who, with funds from La Corporation Culturelle de Frampton and the provincial government, restored the church in 1985. The tradition of the quilt was revived in 1986 and a quilt was created bearing over seven hundred names, both French and English. Signatures had cost ten cents in 1916; they now require a donation of between one and five dollars.

Springbrook was declared a historic monument in 1986 and is used now for cultural events held by La Corporation Culturelle. Each summer, a clean-up bee is organized to maintain the church and grounds. It ends with a community picnic reminiscent of the traditional Anglican garden party. And, the forget-me-nots still bloom in abundance.

St. Edward's cemetery
Second Range, West Frampton.

Here stands the site of St. Edward's Chapel, built in 1826 and closed in 1863. Most of the five hundred and twelve persons buried here were Irish Catholics. In the ensuing years, neglect and pillaging resulted in a wasteland where only two original headstones remained.

In 1991, a local committee was formed to promote the restoration of the cemetery. New headstones were erected to represent each year between 1827 and 1863. Each stone lists the names of those who died that year from the very young to the very old. Some of those names are Walsh, Nugent, Lilly and Farrell. A small replica of the tiny chapel was built and a memorial stone honouring the pioneers who opened up the Frampton area in the early 19th century was erected. It reads: "A Tribute to our Forefathers".

The Frampton steam sawmill
Frampton. (St-Edouard-de-Frampton)

This could be the only operating steam-powered saw mill remaining in Quebec. It stands on the site of the original sawmill which was powered by the Pyke River. There were three English owners between 1808 and 1902: George Pyke, Andrew Hodgson and Thomas Hodgson. Thomas Hodgson converted the previously water-powered mill into a steam mill (circa 1878). The sawdust and wood scraps are fed back into the fire box which heats up the boiler, producing steam and power to run the saws. Water for the boiler is piped in from the Pyke River.

The original mill was built here by George Pyke and Edouard Desbarats, the latter being the colonizer-agent in the Frampton area. Hodgson operated the steam mill until 1902 when it was bought by francophones. The present owners, the Vachon family, have run it since 1923. Fires have destroyed the mill twice (1928, 1941), but, surprisingly, it is still in operation and stands as an important illustration of our industrial past before the coming of electrical power.

The Henderson house
Henderson Blvd. at rue Principale, Route 277, St. Malachy.

William Henderson, born in the Shetland Islands, came to Montreal in 1799 at a young age. He was an entrepreneur in Montreal and Quebec City, served in the Quebec garrison (1812-15), was a partner in Les Vielles Forges at Three Rivers and acted as a land agent.

French-speaking veterans of the 1812 War were offered land south of Quebec City, but most were not willing to leave their seigneuries to open up this new and difficult region. William Henderson bought out their contracts and brought Protestant and Catholic Irish in to settle the area. He developed the St. Malachy area (originally called East Frampton) in the 1830s. His younger brother Gilbert joined him in this venture.

This house, erected in 1843 near Hemison Brook where Henderson built grist and sawmills, was called "the big house" by the family. William Henderson lived to be one hundred years old and died in 1883 in this house. The last Hendersons to live here were William's son and daughter who occupied it until 1925.

The present owner, Paul Ruel, son of Joseph Ruel who bought the house in the 1930s, lives in a modern house next door. Some of his family live in the old house which is in need of repair. Paul Ruel wishes to maintain it as a historic site, even if this means turning it over to a heritage organization.

The Connell farmhouse
1060 Village Road (Main Street), St. Malachy.

Father William Dunn of Kilkenny, Ireland opened the mission in St. Malachy and said Holy Mass for the first time in Timothy Connell's farmhouse on May 11, 1841. The house was built circa 1831 and occupied by Timothy Connell, its likely builder, and later by the Rutherford family.

St. Paul's Church and cemetery
1774 rue Principale, St. Malachy (Hemison).

Anglicans, mostly Irish, were the dominant Protestant denomination in the townships south of Quebec City. Itinerant pastors would minister to several churches in the area, including St. Malachy, Frampton, Cumberland Mills (from 1900) and Megantic (1940s). Until the 1940s, the missionary circuit was traveled on horseback or by foot and the pastor would often visit the faithful in their homes along the way. The first St. Paul's, a wooden structure, was built in 1839 on land donated by William Henderson

and was replaced by this one in 1851. Headstones in the cemetery bear such names as Henderson, Doherty, Forrest and McLaughlin. Most Irish have left the area or have inter-married with the French, although some English-speaking Irish still remain, some of whom speak with a slight French accent and traces of Irish.

The Smith farmhouse
940 Village Road, St. Malachy.

St. Malachie has a lovely setting on a rise over-looking the Etchemin River. It began as a group of farms, including the Connell/Rutherford farm, along this main road. The Smith farm was a mixed operation with milk cows, chickens and pigs. On the porch of the farmhouse built by Archibald Smith (circa 1900) sits Emma Smith (nearest in the photo) – wife of the farmer Roddie Smith, son of Archie – and her daughter Marion. The Smiths, who are Irish Protestant, are among the few English remaining. Marion Smith owns a quilt, created in the 1930s, given to her by Miss Sadie Rutherford in 1960, which bears the embroidered names of many local people, including the Hendersons.

The Pozer manor house

650 de la Chaudière, St-Georges-de-Beauce.

J. George Pozer was the founder of this city which was eventually named after him. The Pozers (originally Pfotzer) emigrated from the area just east of Strasbourg, Germany, first to England and then, in 1773, to Philadelphia. Following the American Revolution, George, a confirmed Loyalist, returned for a time to England and then, in 1785, settled permanently in Quebec with his family. An entrepreneur, he developed two stores, one a successful general store on John Street in Quebec City. He amassed some wealth and, in 1808, bought the Aubert Gallion seigneury, 36 square-miles on the west side of the Chaudière River, in the upper Beauce. There were scattered English settlers in this area around what is now called the Pozer River. As seignior, Pozer built a mill on this river. The first manor house was built in 1830 and this, the second, was built by George's grandson William Milbourn Pozer in 1879. Through marriage, it became the residence of Robert J. Ross and Edith H. Pozer in 1917 and passed out of family hands in 1962. Today, it is a restaurant, Manoir Pozer.

The Pozer family, who have integrated well into the French community, still consider themselves to be English-speaking, with a German ancestry. Like Lutherans in other parts of Quebec, where there was no Lutheran church, they joined the Anglican church. George Pozer died in 1848 at the age of ninety-five and was the second person to be buried in Quebec City's Protestant Mount Hermon cemetery.

The site of the Pozer River dam and grist mill
15th Street, St-Georges-de-Beauce.

George Pozer brought one hundred and eighty-nine colonists from his homeland to settle what became known as "the German settlement". Some remained, but the majority moved on to other parts of Canada and the United States.

Pozer built a dam to supply hydraulic power to the grist mill which he built on the Pozer River in 1817-18. Some remains of this, the first mill in the area to use water-driven turbines, can be seen at the left in the photo. The exit in the centre of the dam was used to control the water level of the river. Nature is slowly reclaiming this site where the seigniory tenants once ground their grain, leaving a portion of their yield as payment.

Gordon Pozer

The Pozer family cemetery

15th Street, St-Georges-de-Beauce.

This is a family cemetery where generations of Pozers and Rosses are buried. Gordon Pozer, our guide, was proud to tell us that the family would not refuse someone who was in need of a place to be buried. Interred here is at least one Catholic who, having committed suicide, was refused burial in the Catholic cemetery.

This is also the site of St. Peter's Anglican Church (1889) which was moved here from the bottom of the hill facing the Chaudière River, in 1947, by Gordon's father, Kenneth Pozer, to be closer to the cemetery. It was, unfortunately, demolished in 1970.

The Pozer family gave much to their community. Visible in the background of the photo is the Catholic church, built on land which they donated. To the right, is a school named after the family. They also gave land towards the building of a convent and a hospital. Christian H. Pozer (1835-1884) represented Beauce in both Ottawa and Quebec from the 1860s to the 1880s.

For generations, the Pozers – big men, well over six feet – worked the land. Gordon Pozer, seen here, moved into the trucking business in 1961, working for Fox and Ginn Transport and, in 1984, started his own trucking company, Transport Pozer, Inc. He dealt in the transport of general freight between Quebec, Ontario, the Maritimes and the North Eastern U.S. He sold the company in 2001, but his logo is still visible at the truck yard.

St. Paul's Church

Cumberland Mills, St-Georges-de-Beauce.

English-speaking people helped to open the upper part of the Chaudière River in the early 19th century. This church (1846-47) stands, ten kilometers east of St-Georges-de-Beauce, not in a community, but on a hill surrounded by a beautifully kept park. In 1911, St. Paul's became part of the pastoral circuit serving English Protestants in the Etchemin River area. The cemetery includes names such as Miller, Taylor, Wintle and Loweryson. This church stands on the route taken by the Benedict Arnold invasion in 1775, which is traveled by thousands of American tourists each year.

The Jersey Mills Presbyterian cemetery
Jersey Mills.

Here is the site of the Presbyterian church (1881-1959). The congregation was formed in 1858 and dissolved one hundred years later. The names on the headstones in this tiny cemetery tucked away in a corner of town are mostly Cathcart, Boyd and Wilson.

The Lower St. Lawrence

The English have a varied history in the Lower St. Lawrence region. Scottish settlers opened up land in the early 19th century in the area which would become Metis; Scots became seigniors in Rivière-du-Loup (Fraserville); the Anglo bourgeoisie left their hot, sometimes disease-ridden cities to spend their summers in cooler, more peaceful places such as St. Patrick (Rivière-du-Loup), Cacouna and, later, Metis.

Summer people were first conveyed to the Lower St. Lawrence by steamship, beginning in the 1840s. With the coming of the railway to Rivière-du-Loup in 1859, and its extension in the 1870s, the summer colonies grew well into the 20th century. The English enclaves were surrounded by French farms, villages and towns. Well-known families such as the Allans, Merediths, Marlers, Drummonds, Molsons, Birkses, Refords and Redpaths came from Montreal and Quebec City and built their splendid houses.

Holidaying in those times was quite different from what it is today. There were no cars. People made the boat or train journey and then stayed for the summer. Where they went, how long they remained, whether they rented, stayed at a hotel, cruised, or built a house depended on their means and inclinations. The pattern began to change in the 1950s: car owners could go away for the week-end; cottages built closer to home allowed more flexibility; passenger rail service became more erratic; and the burgeoning of air travel gave people more options for their holidays. The *bateaux blancs* (steamships) were scrapped or sold as ferries; hotels hit hard times, many going out of business; and as the summer crowd decreased, many of the homes were sold to locals as year-round residences. However, a contingent of the English faithful still return to their summer homes, particularly at Metis.

Rivière-du-Loup

Rivière-du-Loup first appeared as a place name in 1615. The most likely origin of the name is a legend which tells that sea lions (loups-marins) once congregated at the mouth of the river. In 1673, a seigneury was created; the seigneur, Hubert de la Chesnaye created a trading post; and by the end of the French régime sixteen families had made their home here.

In 1781, Henry Caldwell bought the seigneury and built a sawmill which altered the agricultural nature of the area. With the influx of mill-workers, a village grew. In 1806, Alexander Fraser crossed the St. Lawrence River from his Mount Murray seigniory at Murray Bay and purchased the seigniory at Rivière-du-Loup where he then lived with his family. In 1850, the village was incorporated as Fraserville.

The Grand Trunk Railway reached the region in 1859 ensuring its growth. The village became the City of Fraserville in 1910 and in 1919, reverted to its original name of Rivière-du-Loup. A neighbourhood is still referred to as Fraserville. Fraser is a common name in this part of Quebec; for many Frasers, French is their first language.

St. Patrick (Rivière-du-Loup)

The social life of St. Pat's, as the English refer to it, is still the stuff of legend. A distinguished and lively colony of summer people built houses here in the 19th century. Among the well-known residents were Sir John A. Macdonald, Governors Monck and Dufferin and, later, Louis St. Laurent.

Sir William Meredith, a prominent judge in Quebec City, built a summer house at St. Pat's in 1867. His great-grandson Clive Meredith, a former translator for the Quebec government, said recently that, "there aren't enough of us any more. We can only manage a cocktail party or two a year now". He went on to say that it isn't the social life that brings people back, but attachment to the place where you spent your childhood which is always special.

Cacouna

A seigneury, granted to André Daulier du Parc in 1673 and called Le Parc, remained uninhabited according to a 1721 report. Fishermen frequented the area and the first settlers appear to have been Acadians fleeing deportation in 1758. The next arrivals were farmers from Kamouraska.

In 1802, Alexander Fraser acquired the seigniory. He persuaded Bishop Octave Plessis to place the area under the patronage of St. George, the patron saint of England. St-Georges-de-Cacouna parish was established in 1825 and a Catholic church, whose bell was provided by Fraser, was erected.

The beaches of Cacouna began to attract summer travelers who arrived, first by schooner, then by steamship and later by rail. In 1851, about six hundred visitors came to Cacouna; by the 1870s, there were over three thousand. Hotels were built and boarding houses appeared on the scene.

Between 1863, when William Molson built the first summer villa here, and 1912, English businessmen and professionals built more than thirty summer homes and two Protestant churches along the wooded cliffs that bordered the surrounding French farms. Although Cacouna was still agricultural, it had become a fashionable resort. In its heyday, the summer people sent their servants down river early to prepare the villas for their arrival. Now, only a few English families spend their summers here.

The Fraser manor house
32 Fraser Street, Rivière-du-Loup.

Timothy Donohue came from County Cork, Ireland circa 1820 and in 1830 built this house on a hill facing the river. After selling the house to Alexander Fraser in 1834, Donohue and his wife moved to Quebec City where both soon died, perhaps from cholera, leaving six children.

This was the sixth and last Fraser manor on the Fraser seigniory. The west wing (left, in the photo) and a raised mansard roof were added by architect G.-Émile Tanguay in 1888. He also clad the exterior with brick.

Fraser descendants lived here until 1979 when it was sold to Canadian Heritage of Quebec and in 1991 designated a Quebec historic site. The house is now open to the public and serves as an interpretation centre of the life and times of the Fraser family and of historic Rivière-du-Loup.

St. Bartholomew's Church
Rue du Domaine, Rivière-du-Loup.

This neo-Gothic wooden church, with a squared-log interior, stands on a hill overlooking the St. Lawrence River. It was built in 1842 by Charles Touchette on land provided by the Frasers. The Protestant English population in Rivière-du-Loup was comprised of immigrants who arrived following the wars in the 1750s and in 1812 and, later, those from the Maritimes attracted by the railway work in the 1850s.

It is believed that Sir John A. Macdonald, who had a summer residence in nearby St. Patrick, attended this church. The adjoining cemetery is the resting place of English and Scots who established themselves in Fraserville after 1815. Alexander Fraser, who died in 1837, is buried here.

The last resident minister, Rev. W. T. Wheeler, retired in 1947. An annual service is held in the first week of July, when as many as one hundred have attended. The first service in French was given by Rev. William Terry Blizzard in 1979.

"Les Rochers"
336 Fraser Street, St. Patrick, Rivière-du-Loup.

This house, built about 1850 on a rocky bluff over-looking the St. Lawrence River, was the summer residence of Sir John A. Macdonald from about the time of the Pacific scandal (1872-73) until his death in 1891. He set up an office here to continue his political and administrative duties as both Opposition Leader and Prime Minister of Canada in the 1870s and 1880s. Political tasks took place in the morning and social activities, often organized by Mrs. Macdonald, were held in the afternoon and evening. The drinking of scotch whiskey was of course a popular evening pastime.

The view from the balcony is splendid. High above the St. Lawrence River, surrounded by woods, one can bird-watch, whale-watch and spot the ships going up and down river. Federal ministers met here several times to discuss such issues as the building of the CPR and the Louis Riel affair. After Macdonald's death, the residence was bought by CPR president Thomas Shaughnessy. Now the property of Canadian Heritage of Quebec, it is operated as a Bed & Breakfast during the summertime.

"Rockcliff Cottage"
Rue Principale, Cacouna.

Rockcliff, now much changed, was built circa 1865 for Andrew Allan, brother of Hugh Allan. The brothers founded the Montreal Ocean Steamship Company which became the Allan Line. By 1890, the Allan shipping fleet numbered thirty-two ocean-going vessels which transported passengers, goods and the Royal Mail. As did many of Cacouna's summer residents, they lived in Montreal's Golden Square Mile.

This house, in the Gothic style, was likely designed by architects Hopkins and Wily of Montreal who had designed the Allan office building in the port of Montreal. Its distinctive hip roof and skylight are still recognizable. Servants were housed in an annex.

Andrew Allan sold this property in 1876 to Matthew Gault, a relative, whose family vacationed here for four decades. The river was one of the principal attractions at this magnificent location. Residents built bath-houses down at the beach and enjoyed bathing, bird-watching and observing the river traffic.

"Airlie"
390 rue Principale, Cacouna.

Airlie was built in the 1860s by local carpenter Abraham Gagné for Quebec City merchant William Poston, in a style similar to the nearby farm houses. Poston would spend thirty-nine summers here with his family in this charming house adorned with Victorian detail – gingerbread trim along the roof and fancy fretwork atop the dormer windows.

Peter Ogilvie, a Montreal plumber, first came to Cacouna to install plumbing in Montagu Allan's residence *Montrose*. He stayed to serve the Allans and installed

plumbing in many of Cacouna's summer homes. He and his family were so taken with the area, that he bought *Airlie* in 1912. It has been in the family ever since. To this day, the caretakers of the property are descendants of Hyacinthe Lebel, the original owner of the land.

"Montrose"

700 rue Principale, Cacouna.

The climate, vegetation and cliffs of Cacouna are reminiscent of Scotland, a possible reason why the Allan family, with roots in that country, chose this area to build their summer homes. Montagu Allan, son of Hugh, had this large Georgian-style

mansion built in 1900 by contractor Jos. Gosselin of Lévis. The house was renovated in 1913 by architects Hogle and Davis and again in 1942 by the Capuchin Order of Franciscans which purchased it in 1941.

In its day, *Montrose* was the centre of English Cacouna summer society. The Allans entertained many distinguished guests here, including governors-general. Receptions and concerts were held which required the services of as many as twenty domestics. Guests could play lawn tennis, take strolls on the beach, play golf and even attend horse races in the town. They were allowed to play on the superb grass tennis court provided they wore white and didn't swear!

Montagu Allan, a banker, led the good life at *Ravenscrag* in Montreal's Golden Square Mile and at *Montrose*. But, his life was filled with tragedy. He and his wife lost their only son in World War I and also two daughters who drowned in the 1916 sinking of the *Lusitania*. Their third daughter, Martha, who founded the Montreal Repertory Theatre, pre-deceased her father in 1942. Today, this vast residence is a monastery – the tennis games, concerts and garden parties a thing of the past.

The Church of St. James the Apostle
Rue Principale, Cacouna.

Wherever English Protestants put down roots in 19th century Quebec, a Protestant church would likely appear. In Cacouna, the summer residents built St. Andrew's Presbyterian Church and St. James Anglican Church, referred to by their congregations as "summer churches". St. Andrew's closed and was demolished in the 1950s; St. James,

a picturesque wooden church built in 1865 by Joseph Martin, a master carpenter from Cacouna, still serves a small community of various Protestant denominations.

Dufferin House   *Rue Principale, Cacouna.*

With the increasing summer influx of visitors, in the middle of the 19ᵗʰ century, hotels began to spring up in Cacouna: Kelly's Hotel (1850); St. George's Hotel (1862); and St. Lawrence Hall in 1867. The latter would grow to a capacity of six hundred rooms, with grand verandahs which over-looked the St. Lawrence River and a race track. It burned in 1903.

Dufferin House is both a French and an English landmark. Abraham DeVilliers had a large house built here in 1864 which included his living quarters upstairs and a general store on the ground floor. During the summer, he rented out some rooms to tourists. In 1893, Jeremiah Pollock, a traveling salesman, purchased the house and turned it into a hotel. By adding a storey, he increased the room capacity to fifty. This became Dufferin House.

Lord Dufferin, Governor-General of Canada (1872-78), had a residence at Tadoussac and also a house at St. Patrick. The street across from the hotel is named Dufferin, a possible source of the hotel's name. In 1919, Dufferin House was acquired by Joseph Lévesque. His descendants continue to operate it, one of the last hotels remaining in Cacouna.

Metis

Metis (pronounced *matisse* by the English) derives from the aboriginal name "mitiwee", a place of reunion. Mitis, the name given to the nearby river, was the name which the French authorities adopted when they created the seigneury. This area was established as the seigneury DePieras in 1675 and was purchased in the early 1800s by Scots who brought in the first settlers.

With the coming of the railway to the region in the second half of the 19th century, English businessmen and professionals began to build summer houses here. Among the first of these was William Dawson, then principal of McGill University. Many other Montrealers would follow.

When George Stephen, president of the CPR, built his salmon-fishing lodge here in the 1880s, he could not have imagined that his property would one day be home to one of Quebec's most prized gardens – created by his niece, Elsie Reford.

In the early 1900s, there were a number of hotels in Metis which catered to a "discriminating clientele"; by the 1970s, most had disappeared, leaving this little paradise on the river to the cottage owners. Of all the locations on the Lower St. Lawrence developed by the English for their summer homes (Cacouna, Murray Bay, Tadoussac, Metis) this has remained the most English. Along Beach, with its well-kept hedges, stone walls and lawns, the house signs indicate that the descendants of the Molsons, Harringtons, Drummonds, Birkses and Marlers still return to this beautiful place.

Hugh Verrier, originally from Montreal, comes back to the house built for his great-grandfather. He says, "Our family is sort of spread out and Metis is the one place where we all see each other, at least a few weeks every summer." And, descendants of John McNider's Scottish settlers still live here, some of them taking care of properties only occupied a few months of the year.

The Leggatt house
Leggatt Road, Metis.

In 1802, the De Pieras seigneury was purchased by Matthew McNider and, a few years later, acquired by his cousin John, both Quebec merchants, who had the land surveyed for settlement. John McNider, born in Scotland, brought in several Scottish families to settle his seigniory, which stood six miles along the St. Lawrence River at the Mitis River and six miles inland. It would prove to be difficult to farm. In addition to making land available to settlers from Scotland and to soldiers disbanded after the War of 1812, McNider helped them to become established and provided, along with William Price, a base of industry for local employment. John McNider was the true founder of the settlement at Metis.

This house, known as the Carpenter house today, was built by Peter Leggatt circa 1828 and is believed to be the oldest surviving house in the area. It stands as a reminder of the Scottish pioneers of Metis who came here before the summer people.

The Reford Gardens
200 Route 132, Grand-Métis.

In 1886, Montrealer George Stephen, a founder of the Canadian Pacific Railway and president of the Bank of Montreal, had this salmon lodge built near the Metis River. He called it *Estevan Lodge*. ("Estevan" is said to have been Stephen's CPR code name.) Stephen, who was childless, willed the property to his niece, Elsie Meighen Reford, who inherited it in 1918. Elsie, daughter of Robert Meighen and Stephen's sister Elsie, married Robert W. Reford who was prominent in Montreal's shipping business. In time, the building, still known as *Estevan* by the English, would be renamed *Villa Reford*.

Elsie, a self-taught gardener, became an expert in growing rare and unusual plants in this particular micro-climate on the St. Lawrence River. Between 1926 and 1957, she created "one of the world's most beautiful gardens" which comprises 40 acres of trees, pathways and over 2,000 varieties of indigenous and exotic plants. The most famous plant is the Himalayan Blue Poppy – the emblem of the gardens, which, though inspired by the English garden, were born out of her love of plants and of this place. In this photo, we see shrubs of mountain pine lining the pathway to *Villa Reford*.

A woman of great energy and commitment, Elsie Reford was active in philanthropy, social concerns and political causes in the early 1900s. She was a driving force behind the founding of the Women's Canadian Club of Montreal, believing that women should have access to the political and social thinkers and ideas of the day; she was a director of the Montreal Maternity Hospital; and was committed to making bridges between Montreal's French and English communities, by hosting dinners and other events designed to bring together the leaders of these language groups.

This exceptional woman created a horticultural paradise here in Grand-Métis, enjoyed by people from around the world. Reford Gardens has been owned and operated since 1995 by Les Amis des Jardins de Métis, a registered charitable organization whose director is Alexander Reford, great-grandson of Elsie. Today the gardens receive approximately 90,000 visitors each year, eighty-five per cent of whom are from Quebec.

"Birkenshaw"
49 Beach, Metis.

William Dawson, Principal of McGill University (1855-1893), led a group of fellow professors to Metis in the early 1860s. He was one of the first English people to have a summer home built here. Dawson, born in Pictou, Nova Scotia and educated at Edinburgh University as a geologist, is credited with developing McGill University to world class level, particularly in medicine and the sciences. Why did he choose Metis? Perhaps it was the quality of the air, or it could have been the Scottish flavour; as Alice Baldwin writes, "it lies in a patch of heather amongst a vale of fleur-de-lis."

Dawson built this house, which he named *Birkenshaw,* in 1876. He gave the house next door (built circa 1860), to his daughter who had married Professor Bernard Harrington, Dean of Arts at McGill. The Harrington family, well-known in Montreal business and educational circles, still owns the two houses. Other summer people followed the McGill professors, particularly after the arrival of the railway in 1876, and Metis began to rival Cacouna as an English summer enclave.

While Cacouna has declined as an English vacation spot, Metis is still very English. The late Conrad Harrington Sr., great-grandson of William Dawson, had this to say of Metis, "the climate is invigourating; there's swimming, if you can stand the cold; golf, tennis, bridge, and we've got a little painting group. We may be in a rut, but we enjoy it."

The Turriff/Pearce house
117 Beach, Metis.

This house was built in 1899 as a wedding gift to Robert J. Turriff and his wife Mary Selina Astle from Robert's father. It faces the St. Lawrence River and in the distance, on Leggatt Point, we can see a lighthouse which stands near the spot where Peter Leggatt built his 1874 lighthouse. The house had its own water system before there was one in the village of Metis Beach and it still has its original fieldstone foundation, cellar and exterior cedar shingles.

The Turriffs are descended from original Scottish settlers who opened up the land here in the early 1800s. They continued as farmers, owned a sawmill, were involved in the fisheries, and also built hotels in the Metis area, as did the Astle family. In the heyday of Metis as a summer destination, there were twelve hotels here. A Turriff hotel stood across Beach (the main street of Metis) from this house.

Unlike many of the houses here which were built for summer occupancy only, this was built as a year-round residence and is now the home of William and Doreen Pearce. William is a descendant of two settler families, the Turriffs and the Astles. His mother, Evelyn Turriff married James Pearce who emigrated from Scotland in 1913 aboard the *Empress of Ireland* which sank on its return voyage, one of the great marine tragedies of the St. Lawrence River. James was trained as a gardener in Scotland and worked for Elsie Reford as a chauffeur and gardener. The William Pearces are committed to preserving the style and design of the original house while making some renovations and to passing it on in the family tradition.

As we strolled through the village we met two grounds-keepers named Astle and Turriff.

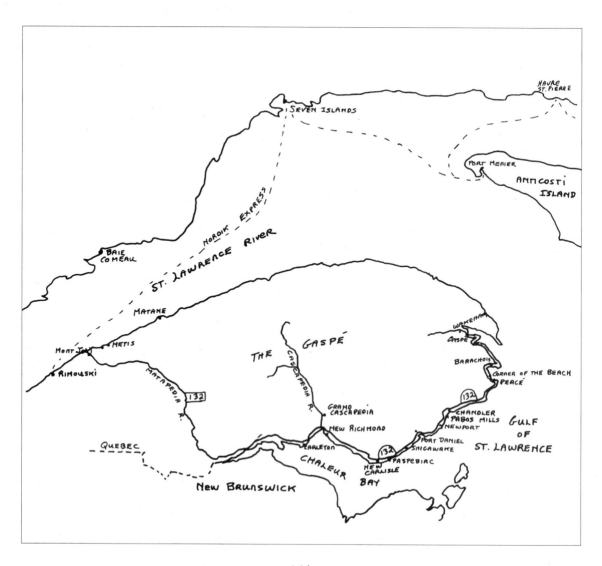

The Gaspé

While the English who came to the Lower St. Lawrence were mostly summer people (except for the early Scots), the English-speakers in the Gaspé came to live and to survive by their labour on the sea, on the land and in the forests. Soldiers from the battlefields of the Seven Years' War and fishermen from the Channel Islands came to this rocky peninsula. The first settlers after the Conquest were refugees: Acadians fleeing British deportation policies in the late 1750s and Loyalists fleeing American persecution. And later, others from Scotland and Ireland arrived by design or by shipwreck. The first Europeans to inhabit the land of the Micmac were French fishermen who remained until they were chased out or burned out during the war with the British.

As we traveled eastward along the southern coastline, on route 132, we came across many of the villages and towns which had been founded by the English, from New Richmond on Chaleur Bay to the town of Gaspé. In many we saw the influence of New England in the architecture. This beautiful region with its calm bay, its rocky shore and inland mountains, was very isolated until 1911, when the CNR completed a branch from the main line along Chaleur Bay to Gaspé town.

Though today, the great majority are French-speaking, in the mid-19th century the Gaspé was forty-five per cent English-speaking. These people helped to build the fisheries, the commercial lumber industry, the pulp and paper industry and, later, copper mining in the region. Now, English and French alike are struggling in the face of high unemployment. The closing of the cod fishery, closures in the mills and mines in Murdochville, Chandler and elsewhere, and the departure from the region of many of the young, for both economic and political reasons – an exodus which accelerated after both World Wars, with servicemen choosing to live elsewhere upon their return – are difficult burdens to bear. Is tourism the last best hope for the approximately 8,000 English (1999 report) and their French neighbours in the Gaspé?

School No.9 and the Almond barn (Gaspesian British Heritage Village)
351 boul. Perron Ouest, New Richmond.

The Gaspesian British Heritage Village, comprising twenty-four historic buildings, was opened in 1989 with the aim of promoting mutual understanding between the various communities of the Gaspé: Amerindians, francophones and anglophones. It highlights the history and culture of those of British descent including their contributions to the development of the Gaspé, particularly in the pioneer period.

School No.9, one of many in the New Richmond area, was built in 1901. Protestant, but not tied to any denomination, it was built for a cost of $449 on the spot on Main Street just west of the Scottish church where an 1830 log school had once stood. The first teacher was paid an annual salary of $140, and the curriculum, in addition to the three R's, included moral and religious instruction, French, geography, history and art. This elementary school closed in 1947 and, in 1950, the Department of National Defense bought the building and remodeled it to include offices and a store on the ground floor and an officers' mess upstairs.

James Almond built this barn in 1850 in Shigawake. In 1994, his great-grandson, Paul Almond, the film director (*Act of the Heart, Isabel*), had it transported plank by plank to this spot and re-constructed. Now called the Almond Centre, it is a facility where Gaspé artists can create and show their work and which promotes the culture of the Gaspé via painting, film and theatre.

The one-horse-power saw and blacksmith shop
(Gaspesian British Heritage Village), *New Richmond.*

Horsepower was one of the main systems of energy in the 19th century. This one-horsepower saw was purchased in Dawsonville, New Brunswick in 1886 and used for about twenty years until farm equipment was modernized, with the arrival on the scene of the gas-powered engine.

This model (some harnessed two horses) allowed for a small horse (maximum 900 pounds) to be led onto the treadmill from the rear of the unit (on the right in the photo). The treadmill turns two wheels which could be connected to a variety of machinery: bucksaw, sharpener, thresher, etc., in fact, anything that could be turned by a belt.

Typically, an entrepreneur would own one of these and travel from farm to farm renting out his services. In its day, this form of horsepower was common along the Gaspé. Few of these machines, in working condition, still remain in Canada. Walter Willett, director of the Village, observed that when the machine arrived at the village, "we loaded up our pony, Micket, and she was turning the treadmill within seconds, as if she had been doing this all her life".

In the background can be seen a 19th century blacksmith shop. There were many of these in New Richmond. The blacksmith was a necessary and respected member of every community; he shod the horses and oxen and made and repaired tools and vehicles. This smithy was a converted 1820s house.

The Pritchard house *217 boul. Perron Est, Black Cape.*

The first contingent of Loyalists to arrive in the Gaspé sailed from Quebec City in 1784. Those who came to New Carlisle and New Richmond were mainly farmers and fishermen with some artificers and tradesmen. In all, between five and six hundred Loyalists came here, joining a small group of Acadians.

Captain Azariah Pritchard, of Welsh origin, from Derby, Connecticut, who had supported the Crown in the Revolutionary War, arrived with his family in the Gaspé in 1783, a year prior to the main group of Loyalists. This interesting and notable Loyalist had, in 1777, been sent to trial for conveying intelligence to the British. He was acquitted by "bribing the presenter" and escaped to Quebec. He served the British as a guide on Lake Champlain, raised a company for the King's Rangers, was commissioned a captain and continued to serve in the secret service until the end of the war.

He sought to settle in Missisquoi, but opposition from Governor Haldimand put an end to this and Captain Pritchard decided to settle at Chaleur Bay. He was granted over one thousand acres of land in Cascapedia and operated at least two stores in the Cascapedia Bay area. He is believed to have built the first grist mill in New Richmond Township. He died in 1827.

Marion Pritchard now lives in this house built in 1888 by her grandfather John Elwin Pritchard, a descendant of Azariah.

The Campbell general store and house *253 boul. Perron O, New Richmond.*

The history of New Richmond begins in the late 1700s with the arrival of Acadians, Loyalists and other Americans, followed in the 1820s and '30s by Irish and highland Scots. New Richmond became very Scottish after 1830. In 1896, Lady Aberdeen wrote, "It is curious that in this parish the majority of the inhabitants are Scotch although we are in Quebec province. There was a ship-building yard just where we are (Stanley House) & some forty or fifty years ago thirteen ships full of Scotch people, mostly highlanders, came here...to find work & they subsequently settled here."

Most settlers, having no money, operated on the barter system which was subject to many abuses on both sides. Many court cases dealt with unpaid debts and attempted swindles. Settlers traded fish, firewood and shingles for such items as tea, sugar, salt and flour. Even church tithes were often paid in goods.

William Cuthbert's Dry Goods Store in New Richmond was a contemporary of this one. An 1854 inventory of Cuthbert's store included items as diverse as: screws, buttons, kid gloves, bonnets and beaver hats and many other articles of clothing, augurs, snuff, chamber pots, sickles, snow-shoes, paint, soap, whiskey, etc.

Today few descendants of those early settlers remain. This house, built by John Campbell (circa 1835), was the general store and post office, with accommodation in the rear. A Campbell descendant still owns this old store.

The St. Andrew's Presbyterian/United Church
211 boul. Perron Ouest, New Richmond.

"To show how Scotch the (New Richmond) community is, there is, wonderful to say, but one Protestant church & that is Presbyterian," enthuses Lady Aberdeen in her 1896 journal about this church which was built in 1839. Settlers gave timber, produce and labour to pay their share of the cost which was four hundred and thirty-five pounds sterling. Of the stiff-backed pews, Olive Willett Smith wrote in the 1930s, "as children we sat very straight and rigid in our muslin dresses. These seats were not more unyielding than the dogma taught us by the earlier type of minister."

Lady Aberdeen, the former Ishbel Maria Marjoribanks of Scotland, was the wife of Canada's Governor-General (1893-98) and an accomplished woman in her own right. She was a founder of both the Victorian Order of Nurses and the National Council of Women and a writer whose journals offer detail and insight into the mores of the times.

Here, Lady Aberdeen gives us a peek at the local churchgoers, "...a curiously Scotch church it is. All the men stop outside until the bell begins to ring at the five minutes & then troop in, & the countenances & attitude of the congregation & the smell of the peppermint strongly remind one of the old country.... Then the trooping out & the procession of vehicles – only these latter are all four-wheeled instead of being gigs & have been tied up round the church during the service. And another difference is that they are all driven off at a breakneck pace." Names on the headstones in the cemetery include: MacWhirter, Caldwell, Campbell, Watson and McClelland.

Also in her journal, Lady Aberdeen writes about relations between "these Presbyterians & the French & the Acadian Roman Catholics," which remind her "of the Highlands". Not only did they attend different churches, they also had different post offices. "Acadians...look down on the Quebec French Canadians & will not mingle with them more than they can help". This was New Richmond as seen by Lady Aberdeen over one hundred years ago.

"Stanley House"

371 boul. Perron Ouest, New Richmond.

Frederic A. Stanley was the Governor-General of Canada from 1888 to 1893, donated a cup "to honour amateur hockey champions" which became the Stanley Cup, and was a hobby carpenter who

helped to build this summer residence for his family. It stands near the Cascapedia River on a point which leads to Chaleur Bay, away from the mosquito and black fly infestations upriver.

The land was originally owned by the Duthie family who arrived here in the 1780s. Duthie's Point was the location of William Cuthbert and Co., ship-builders, in the early 19th century. Cuthbert attracted many Scottish settlers to the area including John Campbell from P.E.I.

Stanley was assisted in the design and building of this house by Mr. Reid, the Government House carpenter who had come from Aberdeenshire. In 1896, Lady Aberdeen described it thus, "It is built of common pine wood & the furniture is of the simplest – plain deal boards for tables with legs of small trunks of unbarked trees....There are eighteen bed-rooms, a nice big octagonal drawing room with a big open fireplace & a brick hearth."

The families of two other governors-general later resided here, those of Lord Aberdeen and the Earl of Minto. Lord and Lady Aberdeen were great favourites among the local people even though Lord Aberdeen raised some hackles due to his choice of alarm clock. He liked to be awakened of a morning by a Scots piper circling the house while playing old Scots airs on the bagpipes.

From 1962 to 1984, the house was operated by the Canada Council for the Arts. Seminars and gatherings for artists and scholars were held here. Much of the original rustic log furniture remains. Today it is the Auberge La Maison Stanley.

The New Dereen fishing camp
Grand Cascapedia, Cascapedia River.

Lord Lansdowne, Governor-General of Canada in the 1880s, had this salmon fishing camp built at a time when governors-general had an almost-exclusive right to fish on the Cascapedia River ("Cascapediak" is an Amerindian word meaning "strong waters"). Landowners with property adjacent to the river also had angling rights. In 1894, the government of Quebec ended the governors-general privilege and opened up fishing rights to bids – that is, people with the money to pay for them. Despite the mosquitos, fishing remains a thriving enterprise on the Cascapedia.

The Vautier lighthouse
Route 132, Bonaventure, New Carlisle..

Jean Vautier, from Jersey, built many lighthouses on the Gaspé coast. Just west of New Carlisle stands this handsome structure said to be the only surviving Vautier lighthouse (mid-19th century). Unfortunately, the records were lost in the big fire of 1964 which destroyed many of the Robin buildings.

The Caldwell house

115 rue Gérard-D-Levesque, New Carlisle.

In 1784, the first Loyalists, coming mostly from the New York area, sailed into what was then called Petit-Paspebiac and soon renamed New Carlisle. Among the first group to arrive was Lieutenant-Governor Cox whose hometown had been Carlisle, England. The village became an administrative centre.

New Carlisle's English heritage is evident in its population and in its architecture which is reminiscent of that of New England. The Caldwell house, built in 1799, is one of the town's original buildings. New Carlisle is the home of an anglo rights group, the Committee for Anglophone Social Action, which deals primarily with the social concerns of English Gaspesians along the coast.

Judge Thompson's house

105 rue Gérard-D-Levesque, New Carlisle.

John Gawler Thompson, son of James Thompson who served with the 78th Fraser Highland Regiment under General Wolfe at the Battle of Quebec in 1759, was born at Quebec in 1787. He was appointed provincial judge of the District of Gaspé in 1827 and in 1859 he became Judge of the Superior Court of Gaspé, a post he held until his death in 1868.

Thompson's house, built in the 1840s in the Anglo-Norman Regency style, sits on a thirty-two acre wooded estate over-looking Chaleur Bay. The property has an authentic English garden, the creation of which was a popular pastime for well-to-do Victorians. Key features of the house are its french windows and its prominent verandah. The interior with its high ceilings and spacious rooms illustrates the stature of Judge Thompson in the community.

The Hamilton house

115 rue Gérard-D-Levesque, New Carlisle.

This Georgian-style house built in 1852 facing Chaleur Bay was home to generations of Hamiltons. Members of the Hamilton family were elected to the office of mayor of New Carlisle and as representatives of Bonaventure County in the parliaments of Quebec and of Canada. They were active in the social, economic, military and political life of the Gaspé from the middle of the 19th century to the early years of the 20th. John Robinson Hamilton, descended from a prominent family in Britain, was the founder of the important Hamilton family in New Carlisle. He was born in Quebec City in 1808 and arrived in New Carlisle in 1830. He had a career in law with the firm of Stuart and Black in Quebec City and is said to have taken the advice of his uncle Judge John G. Thompson to take advantage of opportunities in Gaspé. He was voted to the Legislative Assembly of Lower Canada in 1832 during the tumultuous times prior to the 1837 Rebellion. He was defeated in 1834, but elected again to represent Bonaventure in the new Union government in 1841.

In later years, the house became first a hotel and then a summer residence. In 1983, it was purchased by Doug and Katherine Smollett who opened it as a museum containing Victorian furniture and 19th century artifacts and paintings.

Le Boutillier Brothers fish storage building *Paspebiac.*

The quality of the harbour and the dry winds which swept over the site from west to east, bringing an early thaw along the coast, helped to make Paspebiac the headquarters of the two most important Jersey fishing companies, Charles Robin and Le Boutillier Brothers.

Charles Robin, from the bilingual Island of Jersey, arrived in the Gaspé circa 1766 and set up the cod fishing industry along the coast. Over the years, he brought many skilled people over from Jersey (some indentured for five years) to fish, build boats and run the fish operation. These operations, some of which were in abandoned fishing villages destroyed by the British in the Seven Years' War, spread along the coast from Paspebiac to Grande Rivière and Percé.

This building was erected circa 1850 by Le Boutillier Bros., also of Jersey origin, for storage of the dried cod fish slated for export. Later, this facility was taken over by Robin.

The fire which destroyed many of the buildings in 1964, and the decline of the cod fishery, put an end to the Robin fish industry. The province took over the remaining buildings: the fish-drying building, the weigh station, storage shed, wood shed and carpenter's shop, and has made them into a heritage site, reminding us of the important role of the Jersey people in Gaspé for almost 200 years.

Charles Robin

The Robin Company general-manager's house

Paspebiac..

    The Channel Islanders spoke their own language (a dialect of Norman French) and learned English and standard French in school. They have been British since 1204, when the islands remained under the control of the English king even though the rest of the Duchy of Normandy came under French control. English was a necessity for those in business. Charles Robin, who considered himself British, was educated in British

business practices and was fluent in both English and French, a great advantage in Quebec. The Robin establishment at Paspebiac included a shipyard which produced sixteen ships between 1792 and 1824.

Charles Robin was one of the most powerful figures in the Gaspé and a man of great determination. When a 1787 ordinance from Quebec regulating the Gaspé fisheries angered him, Robin set out by sleigh to Nouvelle; he continued on foot, with Indian guides and pack dogs for his belongings. Robin's 300-mile journey took him three weeks and after three more weeks of meetings and socializing, and satisfied with the outcome, Robin returned in similar fashion to the Gaspé.

Many of the young men of Jersey and Guernsey who came to the Gaspé, and who worked for the Robin enterprises as carpenters, coopers and clerks, etc. married local girls (few Channel Island women came to Quebec) and raised families. Some of their descendants remain here, often a mixture of Channel Islander, Acadian, Celt and others. Those who married Protestants tended to become anglophone, while those who married Catholics became francophone. In 1988, a bilingual group, now called The Gaspé-Jersey-Guernsey Association, was founded with the goal of bringing together people with a Channel Island ancestry. Those who attached themselves to the English community are more likely to know of their Channel Island roots, while many who attached themselves to the French community do not. And in both groups are found those with difficulty in accepting that their ancestors were French-speaking in the case of anglophones and for francophones, that theirs were British. One hopes that participation in the Society can help to alleviate these concerns.

The Robin powder station
Paspebiac.

This is said to be the oldest existing building (1788) of the Robin fishing empire in the Gaspé. Situated on the shoreline of Chaleur Bay, it housed the powder used by the cannons set up to protect the fish plants from American privateers.

The Vautier house

Route 132, Shigawake.

Shigawake (Micmac for "land of the rising sun") is a fishing (lobster and crab), farming and lumber community settled in the early 1800s – mainly by Irish and Scots. Jean Vautier, only twenty-one at the time, was brought over from Jersey by the Robin Company in 1837 to help build boats. Jean built this house (circa 1850), where he lived and died. The original grove of trees still stands in the background. Oral history has it that when Jean was sent a horse from Jersey, he rode it into the house where his Irish wife, Bridget Glenn, was having a baby. Jean's great-great-great-grandson, a Vautier, still runs a boat business in the Shigawake community.

The Le Grand Hotel
Route 132, Port Daniel.

Jacques Cartier visited this area on his first voyage, but Port Daniel, on Chaleur Bay, was only settled in the early 19th century by Scots, Irish, Acadian and Jersey people. This hotel, constructed in the classic Second Empire style, was built in 1899 as a home for Alfred Dumaresq Le Grand, a Jerseyman, who turned it into a hotel which he operated for fifty years. Use of the hotel reached its peak in 1907 with the arrival of the railway which was prevented from continued expansion by the presence of a granite mountain east of Port Daniel.

The principal clients of the hotel were railway workers and their families, salesmen and some tourists. The amenities included a reception hall, a smoking room, a ladies' lounge and twenty-six bedrooms. A slow decline began in 1911 when a tunnel was forged through the granite mountain allowing the train to continue on to Gaspé town. We know that a room cost eight dollars per night in 1940, because Gabrielle Roy, who wrote *Bonheur d'Occasion* in Port Daniel, found it too expensive and rented a room with the McKenzie family for four dollars.

The hotel was abandoned in the early 1960s and became an eyesore, known locally as the "haunted house". After years of disuse and neglect, a committee "Les amis de l'hôtel Le Grand" was formed, the provincial and federal governments provided help and the building was renovated in 1998-99. It is now a heritage site which houses the Town Hall, a library, and a small museum.

The home of Mary Travers, "La Bolduc"
Newport.

Mary Travers, known as *La Bolduc*, was one of Quebec's most famous singers and songwriters of the 1920s and 1930s. Mary was French-speaking, but she had Irish roots. The Travers family came from the north of Ireland to the British colony of New York in the 1760s and, after the American Revolution, they came to Gaspé.

Mary, born in this house in 1894 in the fishing and lumbering town of Newport, left home at the age of thirteen for Montreal where she worked as a domestic. In 1914, aged twenty, she married Édouard Bolduc with whom she had many children. Though not from a musical family, Mary had learned to play several instruments and with the advent of the Depression she began to augment the family income playing the fiddle and singing. Mary's recordings of her own compositions *La Cuisinière* and *La Servante* sold an unprecedented 12,000 copies in Quebec and she was launched on a career singing songs in colloquial French, often ribald and laced with "doubles entendres", about the every day lives of the people. The beloved chanteuse, universally known as *La Bolduc*, had a considerable influence on the evolution of the chanson in Quebec. *The Encyclopedia of Music in Canada* says of her, "Though she has had many imitators, she has had no equals." Mary Travers died in 1941.

Today, there is a museum in Newport celebrating the life of *La Bolduc*. The name Travers still exists in the region.

The King Brothers steam saw mill
Pabos Mills/Chandler.

Pabos was one of the first seigneuries in New France based on the fishery. The French settlement was a casualty of war when it was burned by the British during the Seven Years' War. It was bought by British General Haldimand in the 1760s, whence he introduced the commercial sawmill. Settlers began to arrive who were mainly Irish, but also Scots and English.

In 1872, the King brothers built a steam-run lumber mill on La Pointe de Pabos at the mouth of the Grand Pabos River. They also developed a port for the export of wood products. Following the early lead by Haldimand, King Brothers helped transform Pabos from a fishing community to one with a vibrant lumber industry. In this picture, we see the remains of their mill which closed in 1909 and is now a central part of an historical interpretation centre highlighting the early fishing and lumbering industries of Pabos Mills.

Then came Percy Milton Chandler, an industrialist from Philadelphia, who, in 1913, established the first pulp and paper operation on the Gaspé peninsula. (*The New York Times* was his client). This industry brought more English-speakers to Pabos Mills/Chandler. Unfortunately, the mill closed in 1999, putting 500 employees out of work and placing the community in jeopardy. Recently, the Chandler mill was re-built for the production of specialized coated paper products; however, cost over-runs are dooming the project.

The Robin, Jones & Whitman Store
L'Anse-à-Beaufils, Percé.

Robin developed stores all along the coast to supply the fishing communities. The company has been condemned for some of its practices: reluctance to hire Catholics at the management level until the 1950s (Jersey business people were primarily Anglican) and trucking , which was widely practiced in the fishing, lumbering and mining industries in North America and parts of Europe in the 19th century.

Robin is no longer in the fish business, but Robin, Jones and Whitman, Ltd., today, has three stores in Quebec and two in Cape Breton. The original store on this site, dating from at least as early as 1912, was destroyed by fire and re-built in 1928. It was sold in the 1970s and recently renovated as a Robin General Store museum which exhibits interesting and diverse general store commodities.

Captain Mabe's house
Corner of the Beach, Percé.

In 1797, Adjutant Daniel Mabe (pronounced *may-be*), a United Empire Loyalist from Rhode Island, settled "the corner of the beach". The British government had granted him and his sons a tract of land and here he built his house (circa 1810). The family, descended from French Huguenots who had emigrated to the British colonies in America from Holland in the 17th century, followed the sea – fishing and building boats. They even ran a sawmill which made shingles. These sea captains sailed as far away as Europe and the Caribbean.

Many of the Irish and English who settled here were survivors of shipwrecks. This house, *Le Coin du Banc*, was at one time lit by lamps which used cod oil. It has been run as an auberge for many years by the late Syd Maloney and his wife with "Irish hospitality".

St. Paul's Church and cemetery
Barachois West.

This 1893 Anglican church operates only in the summer now, when it offers services every two weeks. There is still a small English population here and some who return in the summer. Among the names on the headstones are: McCallum, Robertson and Ross, families who were the backbone of the church. The people who first came here were Catholic Irish, French, Channel Islanders and Scots.

Keith Chicoyne, descendant of a Barachois West family, honoured the church and the steadfastness of Gaspesians with these lines in his tribute to the church which was published in 2000:

A tribute to its builders attesting their skill
To date it has stood a hundred years on the hill
If people keep coming through its holy doors
That little church will stand a hundred years more.

The Patterson farmhouse   *Wakeham.*

William Patterson's farmhouse, a ruin since 1919, can be glimpsed through the trees which are reclaiming the land around it. Built circa 1798, this house is recorded as the oldest remains of a home in Gaspé Bay. The Pattersons were early pioneers in the area. John Patterson, a veteran British soldier who fought at Louisbourg and Quebec, and William Patterson, a United Empire Loyalist, were among the early Gaspé settlers. In the early 1760s, grants of land (fifty acres for a private and two hundred acres for a sergeant) were made at Gaspé Bay to British soldiers, almost half of whom had served in the Fraser Highlanders raised in Argyllshire.

Getting close enough to shoot this photo involved taking a risk that we were lucky to weather. The long approach road was blocked by a locked gate bracketed by tracks which indicated that vehicles had gone around it. So, we did. As we progressed, the road became steeper and muddier and offered no place to turn around. Eventually we reached the end, at a clearing which was a sea of mud. We parked, climbed up a hill, photographed the ruins, turned the car around quickly enough not to sink and actually made it back onto the road. Now, the climb back up, slipping, not too slow, stuck momentarily, unstuck.... At last, we made it, drove back around the gate, indulged ourselves in mutual declarations of stupidity and took a breather.

There are still Pattersons in the region. The pioneer settlers of Gaspé town were English, with some bilingual Channel Islanders. The Gaspé Bay area continues to have a substantial English-speaking population, mostly situated in nearby York, Wakeham and Fontenelle.

Felix O'Hara's headstone

*behind 84 rue Jacques Cartier,
Gaspé town.*

"Here lies the body of Felix O'Hara, esq. who departed this life the 10th day of September, 1805, in the 73rd year of his age."

So reads the inscription on the headstone of Felix O'Hara's grave in the tiny O'Hara cemetery which nestles behind a commercial establishment in the town of Gaspé. Felix O'Hara, from County Antrim, Ireland, was granted permission by Governor Murray, in 1764, to settle at Gaspé Basin as a merchant and purveyor of supplies to the British army. He settled in the area twenty years before the arrival of Loyalists, raising a large family with his wife Martha McCormach. He most likely ran a farm, as the 1765 census for Gaspé records his household as including nineteen cattle, and he set up the first general store at "the basin" in the 1770s.

Felix O'Hara played a major role in the early development of Gaspé. He was a justice of the peace, the first judge appointed in the district of Gaspé, and a customs officer. He was involved in the survey of lands and the settlement of new settlers in 1784. He was a landholder in Gaspé and in 1796 became the proprietor of Haldimand's Grand Pabos seigniory. Here he helped settle many Acadians. Felix O'Hara lived in Gaspé until his death in 1805.

"One Ash"
*186 rue de la Reine,
Gaspé Bay.*

One Ash was the home of one of Gaspesia's most widely-known and respected citizens, Commander William Wakeham, M.D. He was born in Quebec City in 1845 to Mary Davidson and George Wakeham, a storekeeper who later became superintendent of the newly established Beauport Lunatic Asylum where he worked for twenty years. William was educated at the High School of Quebec and received his medical degree from McGill University. He set up practice in the Gaspé and in 1876 became the medical director of his father's *Belmont Retreat* at Ste-Foy.

In 1879, Dr. Wakeham was appointed to command the Fisheries Protection Service in the Lower St. Lawrence and Gulf Region. He remained in this service for the rest of his life, leaving his medical practice to do so. He believed he could be of more use in this capacity, though he continued to draw on his medical knowledge and skill when visiting the many outports in the Gulf of St. Lawrence. Commander Wakeham became one of the best-known people in all of Gaspé, Quebec Labrador, P.E.I. and the Gulf Islands. He had an extraordinary acquaintance with every phase of the fisheries: business, science and the economy of the fishery. He convinced the government to provide a proper patrol vessel and became skipper of the official cruiser *Canadienne* and, later, *Princess.* As Commander of the S.S *Diana* in 1897, he sailed on an historic expedition to Hudson's Bay, the Cumberland Strait and the arctic islands, a journey which was significant in Canada's claims in the arctic.

Bluff, handsome, weather-beaten, autocratic as an executive and magistrate, he knew the coasts of the Gulf of St. Lawrence as no one else could. This remarkable man is commemorated in the names of the community of Wakeham, Wakeham Street and Wakeham Bay. He died in 1915.

His stone house, *One Ash*, was built over a period of many years by skilled Gaspé craftsmen such as Luther Coffin. The interior boasted a glass-roofed conservatory, a music room, animal trophy room and sporting room which housed a collection of fine English-made guns. If its walls could talk, we would have a greater knowledge of Gaspé history for Commander Wakeham never wrote his memoirs. Since 2002, the house is known as *Manoir William-Wakeham* which advertizes itself as a "Monument historique. Centre d'exposition et d'interpretation. Patrimoine Jersais et Gaspésie".

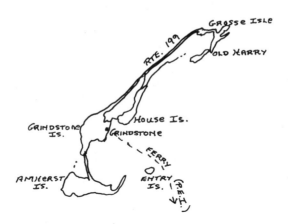

The Magdalen Islands

The Magdalen archipelago is comprised of a string of islands, most of which form the shape of a fishhook. The islands are linked by sandbars and, today, by a causeway and highway. Situated in the Gulf of St. Lawrence, between Gaspé, P.E.I. and Newfoundland, the Magdalens first attracted Europeans in search of walrus, cod and lobster. Many shipwrecks have occurred off these shores; the Magdalens are one of the main ship graveyards of the east coast.

Jacques Cartier was the first to record these islands, on his first voyage in 1534. He named them *les Araynes*. The first grant of fishing rights was given to Nicholas Denys in 1653 by the Company of One Hundred Associates and, later, the islands were granted to François Doublet for the purpose of colonization. He renamed them in honour of his wife Madeleine Fontaine, but he never established a permanent settlement.

After the conquest of 1763, the islands were ceded to Britain, first tied to Newfoundland and, then, in 1774, to Quebec where they have remained. The first settlers were Acadians and a few Canadiens brought by Richard Gridley to hunt walrus. The next arrivals were French families from the island of Miquelon, brought by Father Allain at the time of the French Revolution.

English-speakers began to arrive early in the 19th century. In the 1820s, emigres from Pictou, Nova Scotia settled on Entry Island and Étang du Nord and those from Shelbourne and Argyle, N.S. went to Grosse Isle and East Cape. Between the 1840s and 1860s, several families from P.E.I. settled on Brion Island and Grindstone. The English became the dominant force in the commercial fisheries on the Islands for many years. Once twenty per cent of the Magdalen population, the English now number approximately eight hundred in a population of about 15,000, five hundred of them on Grosse Isle.

Today, the Magdalens can be reached by plane, by passenger/cargo ship from Montreal, or by ferry from Souris, P.E.I. We chose the latter, a five-hour journey which culminates in passage by the rolling green landscape of Entry Island and arrival at Grindstone with its wall of cliffs.

The Henry Clark house
Off route 199, Old Harry.

James Clark emigrated with his family from Nova Scotia to Grosse Isle in 1828, when his son Henry was one year old. Henry, who worked as a farmer and fisherman, moved his family to Old Harry circa 1862, the first English settler there. Two French families were settled there when he arrived, but later left. Seasonal habitation by fishermen went back a long way on Old Harry, but permanent settlement dates from the mid-19th century.

The interior of this house, built by Henry Clark with his son Archibald in the latter part of the 19th century and occupied by them until 1900, is still original and is occupied by Henry's great-granddaughter. Pictured here is her brother Leonard Clark, one of our guides on the Islands. Leonard, who worked on the fishing boats and served in the Canadian Air Force, is a Magdalen Island historian specializing in shipwrecks. He has mapped the location of over seven hundred wrecks, proof that the Magdalens are the equal of Sable Island as a graveyard for ships and their crews. With some training in archaeology, Leonard also researches the remains of the once-flourishing walrus industry.

Of the relationship between French and English on the islands, Leonard says, "I can go anywhere on the Magdalens (Islanders pronounce it Mad-a-leens) and be treated as well as anywhere". Leonard has four children, two of whom still live on the islands.

The old harbour pier
Old Harry Point.

Seen here is the lobster boat *Melody Rick* arriving with her catch and awaiting helpers to off-load. Magdalen Islands lobster is deservedly famous. We had the best we've ever tasted at the Lobster Factory on Grindstone. It is a real factory where the catch is processed, with an adjacent no-frills cafeteria which has long refectory tables. On your tray you can put a very ordinary roll, a paper cup of coleslaw, a tub of melted butter and the freshest, best, steamed lobster you could wish for.

Between 1890 and 1930, five canneries operated on Old Harry. The last one closed in 1943. Many of the fishermen now sail out of Grand Entry Harbour.

St. Peter's by the Sea
Sand Cove Road, Old Harry.

Forests are sparse and tree growth small on these islands and building stone is scarce. Wood imported from the Maritimes is expensive. And so, wood salvaged from shipwrecks was a sought-after building material.

When the Norwegian vessel *Kwango*, on a voyage from Rimouski in 1915 with a cargo of timber, ran aground on a rocky reef in thick weather off Brion Island (the most north-easterly of the Magdalens), the ship broke up. Some of the cargo found its way to Old Harry and Grosse Isle. Local inhabitants salvaged the timbers and donated them for the building of a church at Old Harry. These timbers provided the frame of the church and the balance of the wood came from Nova Scotia. Among the builders were Symond Taker, Colin Turnbull, Wilson Chenell and the Rev. Arthur W. Reeves who would soon leave to join the Canadian Armed Forces in Europe.

Perched on a hill, this, the oldest existing Protestant church in the Magdalen Islands, dating from 1916, has long served as a beacon for fishermen. In 1917, the bell was donated by the Hon. Mrs. Littleton of Rugelay, England. It bears the inscription "Give us peace in our time, O Lord." Many Magdalen Islanders would serve in both World Wars.

The Old Harry schoolhouse
Route 199, Old Harry.

Many of the English-speakers who remain on Grosse Isle and Old Harry are descendants of settlers who came from Argyle, N. S. in the early 1800s. The school was built in 1922-23 and it closed in the 1970s. It now houses a small museum and is home to the Council for Anglophone Magdalen Islanders, whose mandate is to protect English culture on the Islands.

The Keating farmhouse
Rock Hill Point, Grosse Isle.

Our guide at this end of the islands, Leonard Clark, said that he would like to show us his favourite archaeological site. Could we handle a bit of a trek? Sure, we said. Leonard was seventy-eight at the time and was battling a bad cold. Of course we could handle anything that he could.

We hiked for thirty minutes or so on what had once been a road but was now a narrow path overgrown by brush, rocky and uneven in places, and arrived at an open field at the land's end. Beyond, were cliffs descending to the shore, and in the middle of the field stood this farmhouse, now dilapidated but, Leonard assured us, once splendid.

The house had been built in the 1920s by Gordon Keating, a fisherman and farmer. The road was so difficult in winter that Keating moved his family elsewhere in the 1960s and abandoned this land and house which are still owned by the Keating family.

The Rock Hill shoreline
Rock Hill Point, Grosse Isle.

Now, we stand on the precipice with a very steep cliff below us. We must clamber down (and, later, back up again) to reach Leonard's revered site. One of us decided that she could not imagine herself doing either, so Ray went with Leonard. Once down, they walked for over a mile along the shore, over the rocks and through tangled bushes to keep their shoes dry.

Richard Gridley's walrus boiling site
Rock Hill Point, Grosse Isle.

Before the discovery of fossil fuels in the 19th century, animal oil from seals, whales and walrus was a valuable commodity which brought wealth, competition and conflict.

The oil was used as lamp oil, for oiling machinery and for making soap. Walrus ivory tusks were prized in America, Europe and the Near East.

The Magdalen Islands, with their sand dunes and beaches, were a favourite resting place for these great animals. The first to exploit the walrus here were Basque and Breton fishermen. The French continued the hunt until the end of the French régime and the final slaughter took place under British rule. It is believed that the first conflict between French and English in North America occurred over the walrus hunt in the Magdalen Islands in the late 16th century.

British authorities granted the walrus hunting rights in the Magdalens to Colonel Richard Gridley in the early 1760s. Gridley, from Boston, had served as an officer in the British army at Louisbourg and the Battle of Quebec. The rights to the walrus hunt were his reward. He brought Acadians from P.E.I. and a few Canadiens to the Magdalens to develop the operation. He set up his headquarters on Amherst Island (now, Île du Havre Aubert).

The operation was set up on Old Harry, which had proved to be the best location for the hunt. The walrus would congregate on land – called *echouries* – several hundred feet wide, which sloped to the sea. At night, while the walrus rested, the hunters would drive as many as they could onto the killing grounds. The operation had its dangers, as a 2,000-pound walrus retreating to the sea would pause for no hunter; but ultimately, these slow-moving mammoths, trapped on land, were "sitting ducks" for the slaughter.

The blubber was then removed and transported in small boats to Grosse Isle for rendering. Rock Hill Point was likely chosen for this operation because the nearby forest could supply wood for the fires and the deep waters offshore allowed larger vessels to anchor and on-load the casks of oil.

In the photo, we see Leonard Clark pointing to a depression where one of the two drypots, dating from the 1760s, once stood. To the left is a ramp which stood between the two boilers and from where the workers stoked the fires and dumped the blubber into the vats. Here, it was boiled, rendered into oil, barreled and then shipped to market.

Gridley's crews were so efficient over the succeeding thirty years, that this huge mammal – at once, homely and beautiful – was slaughtered to extinction on the Magdalen Islands. The last walrus sighting here was said to have occurred in 1799. Even the bones which once littered these killing fields have disappeared. The only reminder of the Magdalen Island walrus is in some local place names: La Grande Echourie, Seacow Path, Seacow Point and Cape Gridley. Leonard Clark's prized archaeological site is both fascinating and sad.

Nathalie Chaisson

The Grosse Isle cemetery and Will Clark's house
Grosse Isle.

Our guide on Grosse Isle was Byron Clark, another great-grandson of Henry Clark, Sr. (and cousin of Leonard). Byron was born on Old Harry and has worn many hats in his years in the Magdalens. A prominent citizen and former mayor of Grosse Isle, Byron Clark has run a movie theatre in the building where he now has a business refurbishing wooden organs, was a driving force in the formation of the fishermen's co-op at Grosse Isle and is a knowledgeable local historian.

This house, believed to have belonged to Will Clark, brother of Henry, was built circa 1840. It became the telegraph office in the 1880s. Will Clark was a farmer and fisherman (those who did both fared better on the Magdalens). Built in front of the first church on the island (now gone), the house stands adjacent to the Grosse Isle Protestant cemetery which has headstones dating back to the 1850s, with names such as Rankin, Aitken and Driscoll. The hills in the background are those of East Cape in the direction of Old Harry where English-speakers settled.

When asked what he likes most about living on the Magdalen Islands, Byron Clark said, "the air and the peace". Unfortunately, he says, the young who so often move away don't have the same priorities. Asked how Magdalenos vote, he said, "for whoever they think will get in".

Fishing boats, Grosse Isle harbour

Names on these fishing boats include *Can't Afford, Flying Cloud V* and *South Wind No.1.* The language on the pier is English. English-speakers on the Magdalens still use the English place names which are now French on the signs and the maps, e.g. Grindstone (Cap-aux-Meules), Grand Entry (Île de la Grande-Entrée), Amherst (Havre Aubert).

The Acadians brought here by Richard Gridley to work the walrus hunt sold their properties to three settlers who arrived from Argyle, Nova Scotia with their families in 1828: George Goodwin, John Rankin and James Clark.

The Rankin/Best house

Grosse Isle.

John Richard Rankin, a fisherman and farmer who died at age twenty-six, built this house circa 1870. Robert Best, a Jerseyman shipwrecked here in 1871, became a fisherman/farmer here, married a Rankin and became the owner of this house in the 1880s. It served as the post office between 1924-1964 and is now owned by Vera Goodwin, a Best descendant and wife of Byron Clark.

177

The William Leslie house
Main Street, Grindstone.

The first English-speaking settlers on Grindstone Island were Benjamin Turnbull, John Haley, George Flint and John Dickson. They came, perhaps as early as 1805 and settled on the west side of Grindstone at Étang du Nord. Benjamin Turnbull is the progenitor of the Turnbulls who still live on the Magdalen Islands.

The original John Turnbull who arrived at St. John's Island, P.E.I. in 1775 on the *Lovely Nelly* from Scotland is listed in the ship's documents as "run away from this place". Others came "to mend his fortune" or to "seek better bread".

In the mid-19th century, William Leslie arrived on Grindstone Island from Spry Bay, N.S. This is his house, built circa 1880, and now a restaurant. Leslie became one of the island's most prominent businessmen. As in most of the rest of Quebec at that time, the English dominated the commerce of the Magdalen Islands and contributed to their economy. By the end of the century, the Leslie Company operated lobster canning plants, herring smokers and general stores throughout the Islands.

The Leslies were not popular among the fishermen, as they used the trucking system, trading goods from their stores for fish. The family built the local arena, but the old resentments prevailed and the local authorities would not name the arena after them. There are no more Leslies in business on the Magdalens; the only one left has chosen to retire to an outer island.

St. Luke's Church
off Main Street, Grindstone.

It was not until 1847 that the Anglican bishop of Quebec, George Jehosaphat Mountain, became aware that a Protestant population existed in this remote part of Quebec. There were no churches or ministers up to that time, only a few well-worn Bibles. Bishop Mountain decided that, while he was attending to his Gaspé missions in 1850, he would visit the Magdalen Islands. This courageous and determined man set out on his own, traveling in local boats, helped by the hospitality of the Acadians, armed with Bibles and prayer books, to bring the Church to the Magdalens.

His efforts resulted in the establishment of an Anglican mission here and the eventual erection of churches, before the end of the century, in five communities which had Protestants. The first St. Luke's was built in the 1860s. The one pictured, built in 1948, is the third church on this site.

There was never a Presbyterian church on the Islands, but many English-speaking Islanders of Presbyterian upbringing and background attended the Anglican churches. Some inevitably complained about the services being "too high Church".

Among the names on the headstones in the cemetery are those of Savage, Winter and Turnbull. There is no stone for Benjamin Turnbull, but it is believed that he was buried here in 1858.

By 1974, only five Anglicans remained in Grindstone. In 1980, the church, no longer in use, was deconsecrated and is now a centre for Alcoholics Anonymous.

The McLean houses
Main Street, Grindstone.

The McLeans came from East River (Pictou), Nova Scotia to Entry Island in the early 19th century. Some descendants later moved to Grindstone.

The house in the foreground was built by fish merchant Jacob McLean circa 1875; the one in the background (circa 1890) belonged to his son Seaward, a fisherman and farmer. Later McLeans were mechanics and radio operators. These houses were built when the English were at their zenith in the Magdalens – the merchants of the Islands.

Our guide around Grindstone Island was Chester Turnbull, a descendant of pioneer Benjamin Turnbull. (In addition to showing us the English landmarks of his area, he took us to Belle Anse to view the spectacular red cliff coastline of western Grindstone.) Chester, a retired radio operator for the federal government, had a French mother and is very forthright in his views on the relations between French and English on the island.

The main point of friction, he says, was not language but religion. Catholics and Protestants were each obliged to attend schools of their own denomination, and social events excluded those of the other religion. Inter-marriage was discouraged. As the churches declined in power and influence, and with the exodus of English-speakers from the island, divisions lessened and inter-marriage became more frequent. Now, he says, the divisions emanate mainly from the politicians. But even though many barriers have been removed, "the French still feel that the English look down on them". Old hurts die hard.

The Frank Leslie house

Main Street, Grindstone.

The English homes which once lined the main street of Grindstone, belonging to such families as the McLeans, Leslies, Goodwins, Aitkens, Pattons and Delaneys, have all but disappeared, replaced by commercial establishments. This was the house of Frank Leslie, son of William, built circa 1900, which now stands in this shabby condition, next to a shopping centre, perhaps symbolic of the fate of the English in Grindstone. Frank Leslie ran the family business during the Depression which hit the fish industry hard.

The Delaney lobster plant

Route 199, House Harbour.

We met Frank Delaney, an outspoken man, still, at age seventy-four, working as a merchant in Grindstone, at his office. When he was asked how many English still live in Grindstone, he replied, "You're looking at him".

The Delaneys, originally from Killarney, Ireland, arrived in the Magdalens via Nova Scotia, in the 1850s. They became involved in fishing businesses: herring smoking, cod salting, lobster factories. Shown here is an old Delaney lobster plant, owned by J.W.Delaney (cousin of Frank), which is still in business. Frank Delaney says that unlike the Leslies, the Delanys weathered the difficult Depression years by adapting successfully to economic conditions. They also married into the French Catholic population and so integrated better into Island society.

Frank defends the trucking system of the 19th century, as practiced by the Robins (Gaspé), the Prices (Saguenay) and the Leslies and Delaneys (Magdalen Islands), as part of the economic system of the times. Under this system of barter, credit at company stores, paid for by their catch, kept fishermen dependent on the company, making it difficult for them to improve their lives. Frank Delaney argues that in this relationship it was the fishermen who exploited the merchant. The entrepreneurs were indispensable to the fishermen, he says, providing goods and supplies in good times and bad.

The Delaneys were involved in politics as well as commerce. There can be no argument that these English merchants contributed greatly to the development of the Magdalen Islands over the last one hundred and fifty years.

The lighthouse-keepers' house
Delaney Road, Grindstone.

Timothy O'Brien came to the Magdalen Islands to be the lighthouse-keeper on the west side of Grindstone Island. Frank Delaney, Sr. (grandfather of the present Frank Delaney), married one of Timothy's daughters and became the lighthouse-keeper for many years. He built this house on the western coast of Grindstone Island circa 1885.

Oscar Delaney married an Anglican, which, his son Frank says, "kept us on the English side". Frank himself married into "the French side". He has six bilingual children, four of them still living on the Islands. Frank, however, is the only one of his high school class still remaining in the Magdalens. When asked about French-English relations, he was quick to say that there is harmony between the two groups, but "you are thought of as English," and there is still "an atmosphere" between them.

The Pier
Entry Island

Entry Island stands at the entrance to Pleasant Bay, about six kilometres from Grindstone. French settlers once came here but soon left. The first English-speakers arrived from Nova Scotia in the 1820s.

Before roads and causeways were constructed (by 1950) the Islanders depended upon "local boats" to travel between islands. This was their link for business, to obtain supplies, to go to church, or to visit relatives, etc. The boat which still travels between Grindstone and Entry Island is the last of these, which have served the Magdalen Islanders for over one hundred and fifty years.

Fog is a frequent menace here and it sometimes prevents the ferry from making the journey. On our last chance to make the trip, the morning was quite foggy but fortunately the captain felt that it was safe to go. As we arrived at Entry Island about nine a.m. we could see almost nothing. Not auspicious for photographing. We were met at the wharf by our Entry Island guide, Leonard Dickson, who predicted that "it won't lift til four o'clock". He knew that this was the time of our return ferry and we could already see that he had a twinkle. Was he just teasing us?

With the decline of the cod fishery, lobster fishing here has increased. Whereas fifty boats once worked out of Entry Island, now there are only eighteen. Some of these are named *Entry Outlaw, Jenny Anne* and *C.A.M.P.E.R.* Although the island is a prized destination for travelers, it has only one restaurant, one store and one B&B.

Big Hill and All Saints Church
Entry Island.

The hill in the background is the highest point on the island and is known as Big Hill, destination of many visiting hikers.

Bishop G. J. Mountain visited the families on Entry Island in 1850 and 1853. Although the Anglican mission to the Magdalens was created at this time, the people of Entry Island would have to wait another forty-five years for this church. At the time of the 1850 visit, there were eleven families on Entry Island – all Protestant, the largest English group on the Magdalens at that time. A service was held in the largest house on the island, attended by forty or fifty people. Baptisms were performed and Bibles and prayer books distributed.

The first church here was built in 1895. By the 1940s, extensive repairs were needed and the congregation decided to build a new larger church on the same site. Built by local volunteers led by James Chennel who framed the building and John Clarke who constructed the steeple and bell tower and completed the interior, the new church was completed circa 1950. It kept the name All Saints, but would become known as the Royal Rifles War Memorial in memory of Entry Island men who died in Japanese prison camps following the fall of Hong Kong in 1941. Many served; only some returned. Of those who did return, one was still living on the island in 2001.

The cross on the left was erected in 1988 to honour seventeen Entry Island fishermen who lost their lives at sea between 1962 and 1987. The cemetery headstones bear such pioneer names as Dickson, Patton, Welsh and McLean. The stones date back for one hundred years, but there are older stones in the island's family plots – the oldest that of Alexander McLean who died in 1826.

All Saints is still an active church. It has no resident minister, but one comes from Grosse Isle every two weeks. The pulpit comes from St. Augustine's Church in Amherst which was demolished in 1911. One of only three of its kind in Canada, the pulpit is said to have once been part of a ship.

Ivan Quinn's house
Entry Island.

Leonard Dickson, our driver (right in the photo), a retired fisherman, is a descendant of David Dickson the first English settler on Entry Island (1822). The late Ivan Quinn, in his seventies at the time of this photo, was born on Grosse Isle, to a father of Irish descent. Ivan's house, built by Andrew Welsh circa 1883, is the oldest remaining structure on the island. Ivan lived alone here in this house made of hand-hewn beams from Grindstone Island and filled with memorabilia.

A popular guitar player and country singer in the French communities on the main islands, Ivan performed a song for us and posed in his gear. Unfortunately, the heavy fog made the early photos unusable (we shot anyway, mindful of Leonard's dire warning). (A French-speaking Magdalen Islands singer whom we met on the ferry back to P.E.I. spoke of the strong influence of Irish music in the Magdalens.) Ivan Quinn was delightful to meet and very quotable. On the subject of farming he said that, though fishermen once had farms to supply their food, feed and fertilizer became so expensive it was cheaper to buy potatoes and eggs. "Now we buy everything." He said that English and French get along well on the "Mad-a-leens", and some English do speak French, but, "in the past, the English thought they was higher up but they wasn't". Intermarriage has helped.

The Welsh house
Entry Island.

Farm animals roam Entry Island freely, so house-owners have to build fences to keep out the wandering cattle. Henry and Nancy Welsh built this attractive cottage in the late 19th century. It is abandoned now, as are many houses on the island.

Leonard Dickson took us to the near-by local museum which preserves artifacts – equipment, documents and old photographs – relating to the fishing life of Entry Island. It also honours the Entry Islanders who served Canada in the 20th century wars. Leonard gave us a glimpse into what it was like to be a lobster fisherman, which he was for over thirty years. He liked the life, but the worst part was rising at two or three a.m. to start the day. It was a long work day, doing a difficult and sometimes dangerous job.

Suddenly, mercifully, the air cleared and Leonard drove us back to the church and Ivan Quinn's house and the other landmarks we'd photographed in the fog.

"Chez McLean"
Entry Island.

Since Entry Island addresses consist only of names and a Postal Code, Isabel McLean Crowell, the owner of the only public accommodation on the island, had to describe our route from the pier (we'd temporarily parted company with Leonard while we ate our picnic): "go up the road, third house on your left past the church".

186

In the photo are Isabel and her husband Lorne Crowell standing before the house built by Isabel's father, Daniel McLean, in 1927. In addition to operating a small farm, Daniel McLean was the lighthouse-keeper on Entry Island for over thirty years. Isabel, a former nurse in the Canadian Armed Forces, is descended from a long line of McLeans who arrived on the island in the 1820s.

Isabel lives with her husband in Moncton, New Brunswick, in the winter and operates this house as a B&B in the summer. This family is connected to that of Jacob McLean on Grindstone Island. Ardently proud of her heritage, Isabel has developed a mini-museum in her basement of farm and lighthouse memorabilia including a cream separator, juicer, oil lamps, farm implements and the red buoys used by her father as a lighthouse-keeper.

This dynamic woman is a fount of information on the island's past. She has many stories including the delightful tale of old Farmer. Richard McLean, Isabel's great-uncle, sold his horse, Farmer, around 1925 to someone on Grosse Isle. Richard drove Farmer three miles across the ice to Amherst, then up the archipelago past Grindstone, House Harbour and Pointe aux Loups to Grosse Isle. There were no causeways then, so they crossed many stretches of water. Richard left Farmer with his new owner and returned to Entry Island. Farmer evidently preferred life on Entry Island also, because he found his own way back down the archipelago to Amherst where, the ice having by now thawed, he swam home to Entry Island where he was allowed to live out his days.

The Lighthouse-keepers' house
Entry Island.

Entry Island had been the scene of many shipwrecks in the 19th century when a lighthouse was finally erected in 1874. This keeper's cottage, near the lighthouse, was the McLean home for many years. The last occupant was named Collins. The lighthouse disappeared when the cliffs gave way and this house, now abandoned, awaits its fate.

About one hundred and thirty people live permanently on Entry Island today. Except for some inter-marriage, all are English. The population increases somewhat in the summer, when those who winter in Atlantic Canada return.

Why did David Dickson and Alexander McLean leave Nova Scotia to live on such an isolated island nearly two hundred years ago? During the winter, supply ships and mail did not reach this island. Lorne Crowell suggests that the landscape may have reminded them of their original homes in Scotland. Perhaps it was the plentiful fish, or as we so often heard islanders say, "the peace and the air."

Charlevoix

The pre-Cambrian rock of Quebec, one of the oldest in the world, eroded over the eons from the once-high mountains into hills, ridges and river valleys, slopes down to the St. Lawrence River in Charlevoix. The shield has been a great source of minerals and of power, but the land itself has been a challenge for the hardy French farmers who came here. This area, however, has become a haven for travelers, sport fishermen and wealthy summer people – both English and French. Charlevoix begins at Cap Tourmente and ends at the Saguenay River opposite Tadoussac. As soon as we leave the bustle of Ste. Anne-de-Beaupré behind, the beauty of Charlevoix spreads out before us: sea views, rolling hills, rivers, coves, small farms and, in the autumn, a blaze of colour.

When Samuel de Champlain arrived here in the early 17th century, he dropped anchor at what he named Malle Baie. It is said that an unexpected low tide left his ship dry and capsized on a mud flat – so, "bad bay" indeed. The area was designated a seigneury in 1653 and passed between individuals and the Crown for the next hundred years. It was not successfully colonized, but used mainly to supply food for the fur traders in the Saguenay.

After the Conquest, Governor James Murray divided the seigniory into two parts which he gave to two of his officers who had served with the 78th Fraser Highlanders at Quebec. Lieutenant John Nairne named his seigniory Murray Bay and Lieutenant Malcolm Fraser called his Mount Murray. Nairne was the more successful of the two in bringing in both French settlers and Scots soldiers to open up the land. Eventually there was a parish here of five hundred souls, the ancestors of many of the locals today – French-speakers with such names as Warren, Blackburn and McNicoll.

After the cholera epidemic of the 1830s, urban people sought relief from disease and heat and many began to summer at Murray Bay, changing its nature forever. Steamships brought them down the river to the summer playgrounds of Murray Bay and Port-au-Persil. The golden age of this area occurred between 1895 and 1925. Farmers rented their farmhouses for the summer or took in boarders. Hotels sprang up and those who could do so began to build summer homes.

The influx of American and Canadian summer people resulted in development of the hamlets of Point-au-Pic and Cap-à-l'Aigle. A Protestant church was built in 1867, the Manoir Richelieu Hotel in 1899 and one of the first golf courses in North America was created here. Charles Warren was the best-known builder of houses, many of which remain. English-speaking families such as the Bonners, Dawes, Minturns, Tafts and Cabots came here and many of their descendants continue to come.

Affluent French people also built houses here, up the river at Ste-Irenée: among them, Louis Frechette, poet laureate of French Canada; Adolphe Routier, a prominent judge who wrote the French words to *O Canada*; and Rodolphe Forget, President of the Richelieu and Ontario Steamship Line.

There has been a decline in the English presence since the 1950s and the steamers ended their run in the 1960s. A pulp and paper mill developed by the Donohues on La Malbaie River at Clermont still operates. Some descendants of the early summer people still return, but most of the homes have been bought by locals as auberges or permanent residences. Tourists continue to flock to this beauty spot.

Mount Murray manor house

40 Malcolm Fraser boulevard, Cap-à-l'Aigle.

While John Nairne built his manor in the 1760s, Malcolm Fraser continued his career as a soldier in the British army and acquired a second seigniory at Rivière-du-Loup. It wasn't until the 1820s that a manor house was built for this seigniory by William Malcolm Fraser, Malcolm's son. Malcolm had married a French woman and also had many other women in his life by whom he had several children. They were "all taken care of at the time of his death", says Frank Cabot, present owner of the seigniory lands.

The Mount Murray seigniory was bought from a Fraser descendant by George Bonner in 1902 for $50,000. George Bonner was born in Quebec City and made his fortune in New York State. His daughter Maud, grandmother of Frank, married a Cabot. Invitations to Bonner-Cabot tea parties at the manor house were much sought after in their day.

The old manor house suffered many onslaughts in the 20th century. An earthquake in 1925 caused considerable damage, the repairs of which altered the house significantly. Then, in 1975, while it was on loan to Radio Canada as a film set, the manor went up in flames (a cigarette was thought to have been the cause). Mount Murray manor was rebuilt in the 1990s by Frank Cabot and the house was altered once again, although some of the original stone structure still exists. A small lake and Italianate garden replace the former vegetable gardens and fields. The granary, squared-log barn and root cellar still survive as reminders of the original business of the manor.

Frank Cabot must be given credit for preserving this important piece of Quebec heritage. The same cannot be said for the inheritors of John Nairne's manor house at Murray Bay. The last owner, Kitty Gray, left instructions in her will that the house be demolished upon her death. Her motive is not known, but her wishes were carried out and this 18th century landmark was destroyed. The land is now occupied by a housing project and commercial strip.

The Mount Murray granary
40 Malcolm Fraser boulevard, Cap-à-l'Aigle.

The Mount Murray barn
40 Malcolm Fraser boulevard, Cap-à-l'Aigle.

The Gardens of "Les Quatres Vents"
135 Malcolm Fraser boulevard, Cap-à-l'Aigle.

Hidden within the old Mount Murray seigniory repose the magnificent gardens of *Les Quatres Vents*. Conceived by and augmented constantly by Frank and Anne Cabot, the gardens, which cover several acres, are a highly personal marriage of the wild and the cultivated, the magnificent and the humourous. Landscape designs which have evolved over centuries – topiary, reflecting pools, Italianate and Oriental gardens – are juxtaposed with forests, fields and streams, and northern woodland gardens. In his splendid book on the gardens, *A Greater Perfection,* Frank Cabot refers to "a garden rooted in landscape...a bridge between man and nature".

Those fortunate enough to visit the gardens are rewarded by a journey which offers exquisite vistas, areas for serene contemplation and surprises at every turn: a pigeonnier reflected in a pool, a rope bridge over a ravine and a quartet of jazz musicians which are human-sized metal frogs. As you approach them, you trigger the music which emanates from the surrounding bushes. Across the way stand a classical frog quartet who are in like manner persuaded to play as you approach. Gardens are a family tradition, going back to Maud Bonner Cabot, at the manor-house. Access to *Les Quatres Vents* is limited to those who can manage to be included on the list for the few days each summer when the gardens are open to the public. The fees which are collected are donated to an ecological cause.

St. Peter on the Rock Anglican Church *Cap-à-l'Aigle*

The congregation of St. Peter's held their first services in 1872 in a nearby cottage. Next, they transformed an abandoned barn into a church; and in 1922, they re-built the little church, hiring architect Charles Warren, who respected the design of the original building. St. Peter's is still an active church. The Reverend Stuart Martin, who lives in Georgeville in the Eastern Townships, has come to Cap-à-l'Aigle to conduct services for the past thirty-five summers.

"Torwood"
90 Malcolm Fraser boulevard, Cap-à-l'Aigle.

This house, a typical Murray Bay summer residence, was built in 1903-04 for Archibald Campbell of Toronto. It has an unpretentious clapboard exterior and interior walls of B.C. birch. Indicative of the era in which it was built is the existence of servants' quarters. In the photo, the windows have been boarded up for the winter.

The house was bought by the Malcolm Mackenzies in the 1970s and they summered here for many years. Though Frank Cabot has purchased this property (he has bought back a great deal of the original Mount Murray seigniory which was sold over the years), he has arranged with Margery Mackenzie that she may continue to use it for her lifetime. Margery Mackenzie was our guide when we visited *Les Quatres Vents* and of the three of us she was by far the most elegant in crossing the rope bridge.

"Le Barachois"
Main boulevard, Pointe-au-Pic.

George Bonner's father emigrated to Quebec from Monkwearmouth, near Durham, England. He established a lumber business and married Isabel Sewell, a descendant of Jonathan Sewell, Chief Justice of Quebec. Every summer, the Bonners sent their son George to Cap-a-l'Aigle to escape the dangers of disease in the city. From

1842, when young George was five years old, he summered at Beach cottage with the Frasers.

He left Quebec in 1852, aged fifteen, to live with his elder brother John who would later become editor of the *New York Times*. George, successful in business, was able to retire at age forty and pursue his love of salmon fishing. When he lost out to Monsieur "Chocolat" Menier in his bid to buy the island of Anticosti in the 1890s, he was given the opportunity to buy Mount Murray seigniory, which he did in 1902.

George Bonner was involved in the creation of the Murray Bay golf club in the 1870s and in 1898 he built this handsome house on the shore of Murray Bay. This is a Charles Warren house, evidence of his influence by American colonial design. The house views the river from three sides.

The Protestant Church
Rue de la Chapelle, Pointe-au-Pic.

English Protestants were the majority among the vacationers at Murray Bay in the 19th century. By the 1860s, the Protestant population had grown sufficiently to warrant the setting up of religious services in a cottage (over the opposition of the local Catholic priest).

When Anglicans and Presbyterians decided to build a permanent place of worship, land was donated by the Nairne family and the original wooden church was completed in 1867. The builder, Hubert Warren (uncle of Charles), is described as a navigator and carpenter. In 1890, the church was enlarged and in 1909, under the direction of Charles Warren, the walls were clad in stone. This is the church we see today.

Plaques inside the church commemorate notable parishioners such as George Wrong (historian), Howard Taft (U.S. President) and William Hume Blake (writer). Although the English Protestant population of Murray Bay has declined, the church continues to conduct services including weddings, baptisms and memorial services.

"Les Hirondelles"
115 boulevard des Falaises, Pointe-au-Pic.

Charles Warren is recognized as the most skilled builder in the Murray Bay region. He built most of the houses erected during the golden age. He was French with Scottish roots, a great-grandson of John Warren who was a friend of John Nairne. Charles worked and studied in the U.S. He returned to his homeland to design, with architect Pierre Amos, about sixty villas and many public buildings for the Canadian and American summer residents.

The "free architecture" of Murray Bay was inspired primarily by the country houses of England which had in turn been influenced by the tradition of Italian villas of the 16th century. Picturesque houses with clean lines, sweeping roof-lines, the use of local materials and workers and the effort to bring the buildings into harmony with the natural surroundings are the hallmarks of these beautiful houses, such as *Les Hirondelles*.

Charles Warren died in 1929, leaving a significant legacy in the summer houses of Murray Bay.

The Murray Bay golf club

Golf Road, Pointe-au-Pic.

Hitting an object with a stick and throwing an object at a target have existed as human pastimes in many cultures for centuries. The game of golf is, however, a Scottish creation. They introduced the hole as a target in the 15th century and the first rules of golf were written by an Edinburgh group, "The Honourable Company of Edinburgh Golfers". These became the basis of the rules set up at St. Andrew's. One of these rules reads: "If a ball be stopp'd by any person, horse, dog, or anything else, the ball so stopp'd must be played where it lyes." The game of golf was most likely brought to Quebec by soldiers of the Scottish regiments stationed here. One account states that the first known game of golf in Canada took place at Priests' Farm in Montreal in 1824.

The Murray Bay golf club was one of the first in North America. It was founded in 1876, three years after the Royal Montreal and stood next to the grazing grounds on the flats of John Nairne's seigniory. Permanent clubhouse facilities were erected in 1894. Among the founders were George Bonner and William Blake.

An American summer residence
Boulevard des Falaises, Pointe-au-Pic.

The Robert Minturn family arrived at Murray Bay in 1893 and claimed to have been the first Americans to build a summer house here. They imported their own architects, Charles McKim and Isaac Phelps Stokes, who designed two houses for them. The Tafts arrived earlier, but the Minturns built first. This house, acquired by Frederick Osborne and May Minturn in 1975, was built circa 1905 by the Harlan family; they were also Americans, one of whom was a Justice of the U.S. Supreme Court. These houses, built in open fields, are now surrounded by trees.

Americans brought a new culture to Murray Bay. They built bigger houses and furnished them luxuriously. A tradition of afternoon teas, bridge games and dinner parties and a more formal style of dress influenced the summer culture of the area. *The New York Times* was made available for local Americans to pick up at the Minturn/Osborne house; "a little late; but no one cares in the summertime."

Minturns were married in Murray Bay's Protestant Church, among them May Minturn Osborne, a formidable Murray Bay hostess. Several generations of Minturns and Osbornes have summered at Murray Bay. "Even though people come and go, there is strong continuity." (May Osborne)

The Manoir Richelieu
Pointe-au-Pic.

Hotels were built at Murray Bay, from the 1870s, by both French and English. The most spectacular of these was the Manoir Richelieu, a wooden structure with two hundred and fifty rooms, erected in 1899. The architects were Maxwell and Shattuck and the owners were the Richelieu and Ontario Navigational Company (which would become Canada Steamship Lines in 1913). The building was destroyed by fire in 1928 and, amazingly, the replacement (shown here) was built over that winter. It is a structure of concrete and steel with three hundred and fifty rooms, built in the chateau style with Norman turrets. This time, the architect was John S. Archibald, the engineer William Coverdale of Canada Steamship Lines and the builders Wilde and Brydon.

In the 1930s, the Manoir had an 18-hole golf course, a swimming pool (still there), tennis courts, a riding facility, an archery range, a fishing camp with thirty-two lakes (now owned by Paul Desmarais), fine dining, a grand river view and a considerable social cachet. Owners of villas on boulevard des Falaises held and attended receptions and cocktail parties here. Guests came from all over the world. Among the notables were the Duke of Kent, Charlie Chaplin, the King of Siam and Mary Pickford.

William Coverdale amassed a collection of over three thousand maps, prints and paintings reflecting Canada's history. Among the artists were Cockburn, Bartlett and Jeffreys. These decorated the walls of the Manoir for many years. A few remain, but most are in the National Archives in Ottawa.

Business fell off in the 1960s. The hotel was sold to a series of owners; there were labour problems and, eventually, bankruptcy. The Quebec government stepped in, a casino was built on the property and, the Manoir Richelieu was up and running again. It no longer serves as a focal point for local socialites, but caters now to a new clientele. There are some Americans and English-speaking Canadians, but most guests now are French Quebecers. We saw busloads of eager arrivals at the casino which contrasted somewhat with the more sober demeanor of those leaving.

The Donohue house
145 Main Street, Pointe-au-Pic.

Joseph Timothy Donohue had this house constructed by Charles Warren circa 1914. It faces the bay and the river, built before the road which now runs in front of it. The Donohues lived here and also used the house to receive clients for their pulp and paper business.

The house became Auberge La Maison Donohue in the 1980s. Its different architectural influences are pulled together by the uniform use of cedar shingles. The original interior has been maintained, while balconies have been added so that the guests can enjoy the view and river breezes as did the Donohues almost one hundred years ago.

The Donohue pulp and paper mill
Malbaie River, Clermont.

The Timothy Donohue family, Irish Catholics, moved to Quebec City from Rivière-du-Loup in 1834. Joseph Timothy, one of the six children orphaned when their parents died unexpectedly in the late 1830s, built a successful retail business in Quebec City. When the pulp mill on the Malbaie River went into bankruptcy, he bought it and transformed it into a pulp and paper mill.

Donohues ran the mill until the late 1960s when they sold it to a government agency. It was taken over by Quebecor and is today operated by Abitibi-Consolidated. Many still call it the Donohue mill.

"Le Bootlegger"
110 Ruisseau des Frénes, Ste-Agnes de La Malbaie.

A visit to this out-of-the-way restaurant is a journey into a unique and exciting past. The French Canadian-style house was built circa 1860. In 1933, the Turcotte family sold it to Norrie Sellar, an American from Pennsylvania, who had it dismantled, numbered piece by piece and re-constructed here.

Americans were attracted to Charlevoix by its fishing and hunting and in this era of Prohibition in the U.S., by the opportunity to drink and to gamble. The Quebec

morality squad was, however, on the watch for illegal activity and so Norrie Sellar modified the interior of this house in a unique way.

He created a house-within-a-house, accessible via doors which seemed to be walls and secret stairways and passages. Curious authorities could be steered around the hidden chambers, believing that they had gone into every room. Meanwhile, the high rollers and secret drinkers kept quiet until they'd left. Whew!

The loft of the house is now a restaurant specializing in beef and seafood. Bilingual servers keep things moving at the wooden refectory tables. Recorded and live music entertains the guests, American and Canadian, French and English, bus tours, couples and families. Memorabilia abound: bottles, mugs, bills and coins, photos of celebrities – Elvis, Jimmy Durante – and endless bric-a-brac. And, when you've eaten, a guide will lead small groups through the maze: a ceiling to floor bookcase, when pushed, opens into another room; narrow passages and the bathrooms are papered with English newspapers from the 1930s and '40s, "Richard bags three goals", "Roosevelt dies"; game boards are painted onto the floors.

The McLaren chapel
Port-au- Persil.

At the bottom of a long hilly road lies the little harbour town of Port-au- Persil. A hike along the rocky shoreline of the St. Lawrence brings you to the tiny McLaren chapel which has stood here since 1897.

Neil McLaren came from Scotland to Canada in 1812, the first settler in Port-au-Persil. The chapel was built by his son John whose family were the only Protestants in the area. It was served by itinerant missionaries.

Now owned by Rita McLaren Bourgoin, great-great-granddaughter of Neil, who lives in Michigan and summers here each year in her nearby house, the chapel is non-denominational and welcomes all. Twice during the summer, the congregation from Cap-à-l'Aigle joins the small local community (summer residents which include several retired teachers) for services.

The McLaren barn *Port-au- Persil.*

This barn was probably built by John McLaren in the 1890s. The pioneer structure, of squared logs, is prized by the local community. It is a reminder of early farm life in this unusually quiet and beautiful corner of Charlevoix. (Legend has it that explorers gave Port-au-Persil its name when they observed wild parsley growing here.) And a reminder also that the English presence here included farmers as well as summer people.

The Saguenay

The Saguenay was one of the first places in Canada to be visited by European explorers: Jacques Cartier in 1535 and Samuel de Champlain in 1603. An early fur-trading post was established at Tadoussac in the late 16th century. The geography of the area has lured traders and travelers for over four hundred years: the deep waters (Saguenay is a Cree word for "land of deep waters"), fjords, high cliffs, great tides, splendid fishing and, latterly, whale-watching.

There was, however, no gold for Cartier, no route to the Far East for Champlain. Colonization by the Catholic Church in the mid-19th century resulted in great hardship for the French settlers who had to scratch out a living from the meagre soil of the Canadian shield.

Industrialization, increasing immigration and the development of Upper Canada created a huge market for lumber. William Price built his sawmills up the Saguenay River, an industry which provided extra work for the farmers of the region. At the beginning of the 20th century, the Price Brothers and Company, with the American tobacco magnate James Duke, had begun to develop the vast water power resources at Île Maligne near Lac St. Jean. The Price Brothers and Company later began a pulp and paper operation at Riverbend (Alma). In the late 1920s, Alcan built the first Shipshaw dam and power station and English enterprises developed the towns of Kenogami and Arvida.

By the mid-19th century, Tadoussac's role in the fur trade and lumbering had ended. Summer holidayers then discovered this area. Steamers brought them down the St. Lawrence River and the Tadoussac Hotel and summer homes began to appear, attracting mainly Americans and clients of the Alcan and Price companies. Fishing camps flourished on tributary rivers such as the Ste. Marguerite and Petit Saguenay, to take advantage of the splendid salmon and trout fishing.

Canada Steamship Lines steamers ceased their trips up the Saguenay in the mid-1960s, but, visitors still flock to this magnificent river to yacht, sail, enjoy the scenery and to watch the variety of whales.

Although English-speakers are few today in the Saguenay, they played an important role in its development from the mid-19th century to the mid-20th with the building of sawmills, dams, bridges and smelters on the Saguenay and Peribonka Rivers and the creation of a summer community with its houses, churches, hotels and fishing lodges.

The Monument to "Le Père du Saguenay"
Chemin Hôtel Dieu, Chicoutimi

William Price is a fascinating and controversial figure in Quebec history. He has been lauded as a developer of Quebec's forest resources and a significant contributor to its economy, but he has also been accused of exploiting poor and vulnerable French workers via his use of trucking, controlling the food supply, and supporting the Catholic Church as a means of control (a reliable British tactic since the Quebec Act of 1774). Price's biographer Louise Dechêne, in *The Canadian Dictionary of Biography,* describes his monopoly and character thus, "Price ruled the region; charitable when his men were docile, he was ruthless towards those who disputed his domain." (1976). Dickenson and Young write that he controlled the forests (19,940 square kilometers in the Saguenay region), the transport system, the market and labour.

William's son, William Evan, known as "le meilleur des Prices", was fluent in French, with a French-Canadian woman as his mistress, and made his home in Chicoutimi where he was in charge of Price operations in the area. He was elected to the Legislative Assembly, where his election promise was "to protect and support your schools, to protect your religion and your French-Canadian nationality".

When William Evan died in 1880, the inhabitants of the Saguenay parishes mounted a subscription campaign to raise funds to erect a monument in memory of him and of his father. The seminary donated the site and local craftsmen built the fifty-foot tall obelisk using Saguenay granite. The unveiling took place on June 24th, in the early 1880s. The speeches were in French, but the inscriptions are in English. During a time of mutual apprehension between French and English, a monument was erected in the Saguenay by French Catholics honouring English Protestants. Later, the names of two more Prices were added: Sir William and David E. Price. The main inscription reads, *To William Price, Le Père du Saguenay*.

William Price (1789-1867), whose parents were born in Wales, arrived in Lower Canada from England in 1810 as a representative of a British timber firm. Napoleon was blockading the English from the European timber required to build their navy. They turned to their North American colonies, creating an opportunity for entrepreneurs. By 1820, William Price was exporting square timber on his own. By 1833, he and his partners were sending one hundred shiploads a year to supply the British navy.

This was a time of great emigration to North America and a considerable market arose for building lumber. Price plowed back his timber capital into the building of sawmills – thirty-three over the next years on the South and North shores of the St. Lawrence, including the Saguenay. For a time, he was also involved in ship-building; "Like all great entrepreneurs, he was not afraid to think big." (Baldwin). He penetrated far into the wilderness of the Saguenay. New villages emerged with every Price enterprise. In 1825, William married Jane Stewart, a third generation Quebecer, a descendant of a supporter of Bonnie Prince Charlie. They had fourteen children.

The seigneurial land system was strained by an increasing population along the St. Lawrence River and, in 1854, it was terminated. The Catholic Church was losing many of its parishioners to the mills and factories of New England, so the Church initiated a colonization plan to settle the Saguenay region. But, the short growing season and poor acidic soil of the Canadian shield were not conducive to successful farming and by 1861, the 12,000 or so French settlers (and a few English-speaking farmers) were finding it hard to scratch out a living.

Price's sawmills gave the region a great economic boost. They provided work for the settlers and their stores provided supplies. The mills also yielded a ready source of lumber for the building of houses and barns. These pioneers, in turn, gave William Price a source of easily available labour for forest cutting in the winter and millwork in the summer. Families who might have gone to New England for work now stayed in Quebec.

Price set up a three hundred and twenty-five hectare farm near Chicoutimi which employed one hundred people and supplied the lumber camps with wheat, butter, pork, beef and sugar beets. In 1860, a local priest reported that the Price farm had harvested as much grain as all the rest of the parish.

William Price was a hands-on entrepreneur who made journeys in winter to inspect his operations. Succeeding Prices worked first in logging camps and mills, working their way up to management. Arthur Brues, historian of the Saguenay, attributes Price's success to his "stricte probité qui jamais ne fit defaut dans les affaires le plus importante et les plus difficiles".

In the late 1840s, when his mills experienced economic difficulties, William Price did not close them. He wrote to Lord Elgin in 1849 that his workers depended on him for their livelihood. Affectionately known as *le père du Saguenay*, Price learned to speak French and enjoyed singing French songs. He gave one hundred dollars a year to maintain the church at Grande Baie. Strategic or benevolent? A story is told of a Mother Superior who said of the Protestant William Price, "how sad that such a good soul should be damned".

After his death in 1867, Price's company passed to his sons David, William Evan and Evan John and became known as Price Brothers and Company. This company continued to develop a vast business in Quebec's most important industry. The argument concerning the Prices as benefactors or exploiters will continue, but there can be no debate as to the importance of the Price family in the development of the Saguenay region.

St. James Church/William Price museum

1994 Price Street, Kenogami

The town of Kenogami was started in 1910. Sir William Price bought the former Indian settlement and planned to move his headquarters here from Quebec City.

The Church of St. James the Apostle was built in 1912, the same year as the Price mill at Kenogami. The dwindling of the English Protestant population served by the church has resulted in its being sold to Evangelists in 1966 and then, in 1983, moved across the road to this English-style park for use as a museum illustrating the history of pulp and paper in the Lac St. Jean region and the role of the Prices. Today, Kenogami is part of the larger municipality of Saguenay.

"Villa Price", the William Price guest house

3884 rue Alonzo-Gravel, Kenogami

Villa Price was built in 1911 for the third William Price who, later, became Sir William. He lived here three years and then, in 1915, he built *Cascade,* nearby, which became his main residence. The first house became his guest house, a place to welcome company visitors. It overlooks the Rivière-aux-Sables which flows into the Saguenay, not far from the mill. The nearby park is surrounded by mill managers' houses.

William was born in Chile, son of Henry and grandson of the first William Price. Henry was persuaded to return to Canada, as the other Prices were without legal heirs. By the turn of the century, William III was running the company.

Cascade is now an apartment house and *Villa Price* has become *Auberge Pachon*, renovated respecting its original state. A large map in one dining room illustrates the considerable forest holdings of Price Brothers in Quebec.

William Price Park

Price Street, Kenogami

The rain-swollen Saguenay River was raging. The year was 1924 and Sir William's son Arthur Clifford, called "Coosie", was now with the Company at Chicoutimi. He asked his father to come up from Quebec City to assess the situation. Sir William was observing the river from a hillside when the ground gave way and he was swept to his death below.

Friends created a park in his memory on land over-looking the Price mill and not far from the guest house. Sir William, who had been given a knighthood in 1915 for setting up the Valcartier training camp, was buried here. The park is currently closed to the public.

The Church of St. Andrew and St. John
3848 King George Street, Kenogami

This is now the only church in the region which serves English Protestants. The waxing and subsequent waning of the requirement for churches here is an apt illustration of the growth and decline of the English population.

During the early 1920s, the Presbyterians of Kenogami held their services in the nearby Price Company Club House. In 1926, this building, an unused schoolhouse owned by the Price Company, was moved from the bank of the Saguenay River to this spot in Kenogami where it became the Kenogami United Church and, in 1952, was re-named St. Andrew's United Church. With the closings of the other Protestant churches – St. James (Kenogami), St. George's (Arvida) and St. John's (Arvida) – this has become the sole surviving Protestant church. Since 1971, it has held a shared ministry, Anglican and United, and now serves many denominations. Since 1994, the church has operated with lay leadership under the name of the Church of St. Andrew and St. John.

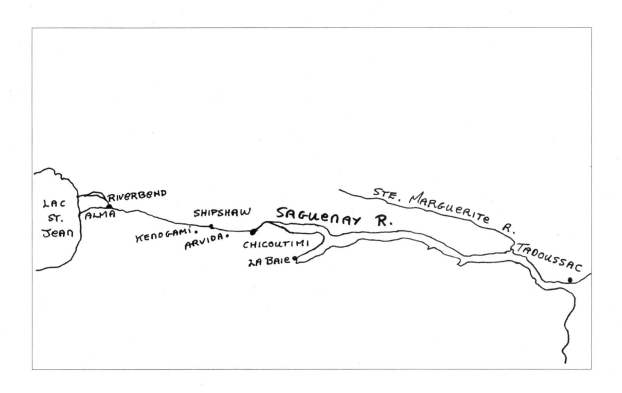

The Saguenay Inn
1655 Powell Street, Arvida

Arvida was a company town. Its name derives from that of Arthur Vining Davis, an American pioneer in the development of aluminum. Alcan built houses for its married staff in the 1920s and 1930s. At the end of the thirties, President R.E. Powell undertook to build a facility to house young single employees. He hired the Montreal firm of Featherstonhaugh and Dunford and contractor J. L. E. Price. In 1939-40, they erected this replica of a Norman castle with Canadien embellishments: a curved roof and joints typical of early Quebec houses. The interior was elaborately decorated since, in addition to housing employees, the inn also hosted business meetings. In the early 1950s, residents began building their own homes and the company opened the hotel to the community. It became a gathering spot for townspeople offering musical performances, dances with full orchestra and outdoor sports.

The interior reflected the sources of Alcan's product by using Huba Balli wood from British Guyana where the bauxite was mined and knotty pine from Quebec where the aluminum was smelted. Other details included a slate entry floor, aluminum staircase and marble fittings. Artwork decorated the walls. Celebrities received here

included Maurice Chevalier, Charles Aznavour, Queen Elizabeth and Prince Philip, Robert Bourassa and various ambassadors.

A 1952 plaque, on an exterior wall, commemorates Simon Ross "the first settler, about 1841, on land adjoining the Saguenay Inn".

By the mid-1980s the hotel was struggling. Labour problems exacerbated the situation and Alcan decided to exit the hotel business. After it closed in 1985, the company considered many uses for the building: a seniors' home, commercial hotel or an arts centre. They eventually set up an Alcan training centre here, perhaps a come-down for this handsome building. The "wonderful years" of the fifties and sixties are now distant memories.

Company houses for English workers
Deville Street, Arvida

Arvida was built by American capital in the 1920s. The Alcan Company committed itself to build each worker family a detached house with a garden. The Deville Street houses were within walking distance of the Alcan plant. Company housing was superior to Quebec village houses of the time, offering indoor plumbing and electricity.

There was, however, a downside to these benefits. The company ruled the town, choosing the mayor and councillors, exercising social control with rules such as "no sale of alcohol within the town". The first large building was a jail.

These houses are no longer occupied by English workers. Company control has waned. As elsewhere, the English population has shrunk drastically, but they built well and the buildings remain.

The Brittany apartments
1911-2911 Brittany Street, Arvida

These handsome houses were erected at the same time as the Saguenay Inn and designed by the same architect. Another Alcan project, they were built to house families until detached housing was available. They are still owned by Alcan and are rented by company retirees.

St. John of the Saguenay United Church
2885 Berthier, Arvida

By the end of the 1930s, Arvida had a population of ten thousand, the majority of whom were English-speakers. This church, originally called Arvida First United, built in 1950, and the Anglican church next door indicate the prominence of English Protestants in Arvida at that time. In 1974, the Anglican congregation joined this church in a shared ministry. Today, perhaps one hundred English remain in Arvida. The nearby English school, Riverside, an amalgamation of Saguenay Valley School (Protestant) and St. Patrick's School (English Catholic), is said to have a student population which is less than five per cent English. The Anglican church is now French Pentecostal and this church, since 1993, French Baptist, striking evidence of the decline of the English.

The Grande Baie Protestant cemetery
Rue Alexis-Simard, La Baie

Old maps show the community of Grande Bay. "Ha-Ha" is said to be an old aboriginal expression meaning "a path in the woods". Among the names on the headstones here are those of William Blair, who died in 1846 (the oldest stone), the Purves family and Robert Blair.

Robert Blair was an agronomist who emigrated from Scotland in 1831. In 1842, he was hired by William Price to establish a settlement at Grande Baie; to get there he undertook a journey most unusual in its mode of transport. According to Jean Provencher in his book *Les Quatres Saisons*, Blair traveled from Quebec to Ha-Ha Bay by horse-boat. This was a vessel propelled by four horses walking a treadmill which was connected to paddle-wheels. Such vessels were fairly common at this time for use as short-haul ferries, but to have traveled the distance that Robert Blair did was risky, but imaginative. This way he was able to bring all his goods with him, including horses. He established a successful farm here for William Price which became the year-round base for the company's timber operations in the Saguenay. Robert Blair died at Grande Baie in 1870. Many of his workers are also buried here.

The Abitibi-Price paper mill, *Riverbend (Alma)*

Sir William Price expanded Price Brothers and Company to include pulp and paper. The Kenogami newsprint mill was built in 1912. James Duke, realizing the increasing need for power in the 1920s, constructed a power plant at Île Maligne, near Alma. The Price Brothers and Company then built the newsprint mill to take advantage of the discharge from Lac St. Jean close to the power plant. It was the first all-electrically operated mill in North America.

Sir William's son Arthur Clifford (1900-82), would become the last family president of the company. Family ownership ended during the Depression, but he returned prior to World War II to run the company and become its president. In the late 1970s the company was bought by Abitibi Paper and became known as Abitibi-Price. This sign remains, though the company is now Abitibi-Consolidated.

Riverbend homes

These company houses, in the English style, were built to house senior staff. They stand in a pleasant secluded area of Alma. Today, they are privately owned by French-speakers.

Row houses

at Mahoney Street and McNaughton Avenue, Riverbend (Alma)

Price Brothers built a company hotel for the use of superintendents and these more modest company houses, also in the English style, were built for the workers. The owners are now French-speaking, but some of the streets retain their original names: Price, McNaughton, Mahoney.

The Bardsville and Ste. Marguerite fishing camps
Ste. Marguerite River near Sacre Coeur.

Scots and Englishmen were extremely prominent in introducing the sport of fly-fishing to Quebec. The Ste. Marguerite River, just west of Tadoussac, famous for its salmon and trout, once drew princes and millionaires to fly-fish its waters. These camps were both built in the mid 19th century, Bardsville in the 1860s. Dates scribbled on the interior walls at Bardsville by visiting fishermen include 1865, 1880 and 1889. This cabin, still in use, can accommodate ten. Bunk beds, a fireplace and a kitchen are among its amenities. The steep-pitched roof keeps off the snow, important since the campsite is closed in winter.

Fishing on the Ste. Marguerite is not what it once was. Poaching, over-fishing in the Atlantic, unchecked netting and easy access by car have all contributed to a depletion of the stock.

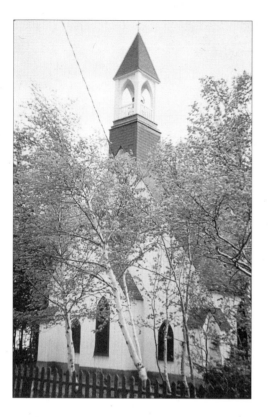

The Protestant chapel
Rue des Pionniers. Tadoussac

Built in 1868, this chapel founded by Anglicans and Presbyterians, was open to all Protestant denominations. Among the founders were John Redpath and William Dawson of Montreal, William Rhodes of Quebec City and John McLaren of Port-au-Persil.

Bronze plaques, commemorating members of the congregation, adorn the wide pine boards of the interior walls of this wooden church. Instead of pews, seating consists of individual wooden chairs. There has never been an Easter or Christmas service held here in this church which serves the summer population.

The Tadoussac Hotel
165 rue Bord-de-l'Eau.

Canada's first fur-trad-ing post was at Tadoussac, beginning in 1600. It then became a real French settlement with a few farms. During the British regime a Hudson's Bay Company post was established here.

English-speakers discovered Tadoussac as a summer resort in the 1860s. Affluent people from Quebec City and Montreal built homes here and, in 1864, the wooden

Tadoussac Hotel was erected. Canada Steamship Lines steamers made Tadoussac accessible and, later, route 138 and the river ferry brought the summer visitors and residents. The hotel was the centre of summer village life, with Canadians and Americans arriving by steamer for a stay of one week to two months.

In 1941, the hotel was destroyed by fire and replaced in 1942 by Canada Steamship Lines, under the presidency of William Hugh Coverdale, with the present building. The activities engaged in by the clientele included fishing, golf, tennis, swimming, dances, concerts and sight-seeing. The decor featured Canadiana furniture and prints by such artists as Cornelius Kriegoff and Paul Kane. The staff, until the 1960s, consisted of a mix of village people and English university students.

Saguenay River cruises ceased in the mid-sixties. Today, the hotel is owned by the Dufour group which uses local staff and draws a mix of English and French visitors staying, as a rule, for shorter stays than those in the past. Whale-watching and day-trip Saguenay cruises are the main attractions. The Canadiana furniture and paintings are gone, TVs replace the concerts, the tea room is now a bar and shorts and jeans replace the blazers and ties of the past.

"Fletcher Cottage"
Rue Bord-de-l'Eau, Tadoussac

One of the first to build a summer home here was Colonel William Rhodes, from Quebec City, who brought his family to Tadoussac in the 1860s. Apparently, among their accouterments were two cows which they brought with them and grazed nearby. Summer residents arrived with a great deal of baggage after a long trek, but they then stayed for the whole summer.

Fletcher Cottage was named for Colonel Fletcher, aide-de-camp to Lord Dufferin. It was renovated for Fletcher in 1873 and later became the summer residence of Sir William Price and his wife. The original part of the house, to which much has been added, is the centre part. Today, it belongs to Bill Glassco, a grandson of Sir William. Some of the original 19th century families, with names such as Rhodes, Evans, Price, Beattie, Morewood, Stairs, Smith and Stevenson, continue to return to Tadoussac.

"Dufferin House"
Tadoussac Bay.

Frederick Temple, Lord Dufferin (Governor-General of Canada 1872-78), and his wife did not take long in deciding to build at Tadoussac. In 1872, Lady Dufferin wrote "not only as tourists, but as sailors, we are delighted with it."

Another inducement was likely the purchase price of the land. Lord Dufferin bought it from the federal government for one dollar. The house, similar in style to houses built by the British in India, was constructed in sections in Quebec City and shipped on "goelettes" to Tadoussac where it was assembled on the edge of a cliff with a marvellous view of Tadoussac Bay (on the left of the photo). The presence of the Governor-General likely influenced others to summer in Tadoussac.

The Tadoussac Tennis Club
Rue des Pionniers.

The roots of tennis go back to 12th century France where a kind of handball was played in castle courtyards (thus, tennis "courts") and monastery cloisters. The raquet was introduced around 1500 and Major Walter Wingfield is credited with inventing outdoor lawn tennis in England, where he published the rules in 1873. Soon after, the game was imported to Canada. It is believed that the first tennis tournament in Canada took place at the Montreal Cricket Club in 1878. Tennis has become very popular in the province of Quebec and is played by both French and English.

Among the founders of the tennis and croquet club at Tadoussac in 1909 were Mrs. William Price, Leslie Russell and a Mrs. Evans. In 1912, a small log cabin clubhouse with a fireplace, a wood-burning stove and a tiny kitchen, was built.

The tennis facilities consisted of three clay-surfaced courts: two upper courts and this lower one. It was a social centre for the English of Tadoussac, young and old. Famous for its Friday "tennis teas", the club was a summer tradition for all cottagers. Tennis whites were mandatory, but now colours are permitted.

The North Shore

Traveling the North Shore from Tadoussac to Seven Islands, by car down route 138, along the whale route, we are treated to vistas of the Gulf of St. Lawrence, of tumbling rivers and the wild rugged terrain of the Canadian shield.

This is the home of the Montagnais peoples, site of early French fishing and whaling villages and fur-trading posts which operated from the 17th century until the middle of the 19th century. Jesuit and Recollet missions were established here in the 17th century and the occasional sawmill was built in the 19th century in this area where the climate and soil were so inhospitable to farming.

This area's forests and rivers and minerals were first exploited by English-speakers in the 20th century. There were five communities where English entrepreneurs made an impact. First, at the turn of the century, came the Clarke family of Ontario, to establish a pulp operation at Clarke City, near Seven Islands. Then, Colonel R. R. McCormick, from Chicago, established a pulp operation at Shelter Bay (Port Cartier). This became Quebec North Shore Pulp and Paper Company, which in the 1930s established a pulp and paper operation at Baie Comeau. An aluminum operation came later. Anglo-Canadian Co. set up a pulp mill at Forestville and, finally, at Seven Islands, in the 1950s, the Iron Ore Company began its mining and railway operations.

Out of the wilderness, towns and cities grew around rough rivers – the Marguerite (Clarke City), Rivière-aux-Rochers (Shelter Bay), the Manicouagan (Baie Comeau) and Sault-au-Cauchon (Forestville) – which entered the Gulf from the Canadian shield. English engineers and entrepreneurs had brought industrialization to the North Shore.

The English, so dominant in those early years, are struggling to survive here now, except at Seven Islands. English schools have a difficult time maintaining their traditions since the vast majority of their students are French. However, in Seven Islands there is an English school with a predominantly English student body, a rare occurrence outside the major cities in 21st century Quebec.

The flume
1ˢᵗ Avenue, Forestville

Forestville was founded in 1937 thanks to the development of hydro-electric power and forest wealth by Anglo-Canadian Pulp and Paper. The village was named for Irishman Grant W. Forrest, manager of the first sawmill set up in 1845 at the mouth of the Sault-au-Cauchon River. Logs from the forests of the interior floated down the Sault-au-Cauchon to a holding station near the dam. From here they were washed down the flume to the quay where they were loaded onto ships and transported to Quebec City for processing. Among the companies here were Anglo-Canadian Pulp & Paper Mills Ltd., in the 1930s; later, the Reed Company; and, finally, the Japanese company Daishowa who closed it in 1993.

Few may remember the Quebec Aces hockey team but most know the name of Jean Beliveau who played for this team before he became a Montreal Canadien. The Aces were named for the Anglo-Canadian Employees Society in Quebec City.

Trinity Anglican Church
2 Second Street, Forestville

English-language services began on an ad hoc basis in Forestville in1945 and, in 1955, Trinity Church was dedicated by Archbishop Carrington. The church had a short history, having been closed in 1979 just a few months short of its 25th anniversary. For most of its existence Trinity Church was served on a monthly basis by the rector of Baie Comeau with occasional additional services. Periods of more regular ministry occurred from 1970-72 when the Rev. Ruth Matthews conducted a weekly service and a Sunday school and from 1975 under the Rev. Rufus Onyewuchi. It is now home to la Petite Musée de l'Anglicaine which illustrates the pulp industry in Forestville.

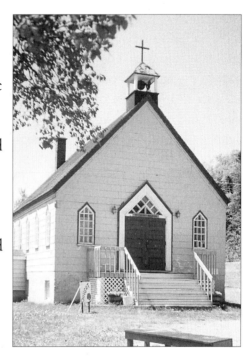

The Colonel R. McCormick memorial statue

Place du Col. McCormick, Baie Comeau

Col. McCormick (1880-1955) is considered to have been the founder of Baie Comeau. This imposing man, who stood 6'4", explored the North Shore from 1915 looking for sources of power to run mills and for forest resources to produce newsprint for his newspaper, *The Chicago Tribune*. He was president of this newspaper from 1911 and sole editor and publisher from 1925.

In 1936, a party of engineers landed in the Baie Comeau area and found only a wharf and five small weather-beaten buildings which the company had erected a few years earlier. The company had obtained cutting rights from Premier Duplessis, and twenty months after their arrival the first roll of newsprint produced on the North Shore came off machine No.1. A planned town grew up on this site. "History is built on dreams, practical dreams of practical men." (Arthur Schmon)

In this wilderness there was no road or rail access to the rest of Quebec. The only route was by water. The power developed by McCormick's company, Quebec North Shore Pulp & Paper Co., influenced others such as the British Aluminum Company and Cargill to establish in Baie Comeau, which today is a city of 25,000.

Originally run by English management, with French blue collar workers, the company today, Abitibi-Consolidated, has French managers. All those hired must speak

French and not necessarily English although, since the company is international, upper management must be bilingual.

Col. McCormick (he served in the American army during World War I) has been described as conservative and isolationist. "Harsh and money-grubbing, he used his newspapers to foment his own rabble-rousing agenda." (Richard N. Smith) Smith saw McCormick's stand against Roosevelt's policies as helping to doom the League of Nations. He also believed that the character of Charles Foster Kane, of Orson Welles' *Citizen Kane*, usually said to have been based on William Randolph Hearst, was more likely a composite of Hearst, utilities magnate Samuel Insull and Col. McCormick.

This genuine eccentric, who never let his eccentricity get in the way of his lust for power and money, played a dominant role in the early development of Quebec's North Shore. This bronze statue designed by Wheeler William in 1956 and a large mural in Baie Comeau's downtown centre were erected in recognition of this by the people of Baie Comeau.

Quebec North Shore upper management houses
Champlain Street,
Baie Comeau

This was once the "English quarter" of Baie Comeau. These houses, over-looking the bay, were built by the company for English managers and staff. The mill (today, Abitibi) can be seen in the background. English churches and schools stood nearby and The Manoir was next door. The Benedict Mulroney family spent several years in a modest house on this street. Few English remain in Baie Comeau today.

The Manoir
8 Cabot Avenue (off Champlain Street), Baie Comeau

The first Manoir, built in 1938, was erected by Quebec North Shore to house company staff and teachers and built in an elegant style to attract businessmen to this isolated area. It was constructed of wood with a pitched roof and dormer windows. That building was destroyed by fire in 1965 and this one built in the French style, of stone, with towers, replaced it in 1968. It is now a hotel, Hotel Le Manoir, which over-looks the bay and the St. Lawrence River.

The former English Protestant school
Baie Comeau

A unique feature of the old section of Baie Comeau is the large historic murals painted on some building walls. This one depicts a classroom scene and appears on the first Protestant school, built in 1939. This school later became a library, and is now a cultural centre. English Protestants merged with English Catholics in the old Catholic elementary school in 1973. Now only one English school remains. It is called Baie Comeau High School (it also incorporates an elementary school), and its language of instruction is English, but the student body is ninety-eight per cent French. Most, however, speak no English at home, making it difficult for teachers to develop and protect English traditions and culture. We heard only French spoken in the school-yard. The sole English institutions remaining in Baie Comeau are this school, the church and the Boy Scouts.

The Alice Lane municipal library
6 Radisson Ave, Baie Comeau

This is considered to have been the first bilingual library in Quebec. Alice Lane, wife of the first mill manager, an American, Jim Lane (1938), was a pioneer in the development of culture in Baie Comeau and was the driving force in setting up the town's first library.

This city, which is almost totally French-speaking, chose to remember this English patron of culture by naming its municipal library in her honour.

Stained-glass windows of the Church of St. Andrew and St. George
34 Carlton Ave, Baie Comeau

Ti-Basse was a Montagnais who saved the life of Col. McCormick. In 1915, McCormick and his guide Roméo Parent were exploring in the area of Shelter Bay when they encountered a violent storm. Lost, exhausted and running out of supplies, they fired shots in the air. Ti-Basse, nearby on his hunting grounds, heard the shots and brought the two exhausted men to his living quarters where he tended them until they were well enough and then showed them the way back home.

Col. McCormick would never forget Ti-Basse. He provided him with provisions and ammunition and when his house burned, McCormick had it rebuilt for him. Ti-Basse gave practical information on the natural surroundings to the engineers who were constructing the operations at Shelter Bay.

In the 1940s, Col. McCormick donated a stained-glass window to this church in memory of his wife. It depicts a Nativity scene, North Shore version. Clara Fargo Thomas designed this Madonna and Child surrounded by moose, caribou, a bear, a wolf, an ox, a dove, an eagle, a salmon, and – there among them – Ti-Basse, preserved and honoured for posterity.

St. Andrew and St. George, originally Anglican, was the first church built in the area (1937). From the beginning, it has had an open policy towards other religions. Still an active church, with a Tudor-style interior and the original oak pews, it hosts a service every three weeks. The last full-time minister left in 1982. The congregation now numbers only thirty or forty, with an average attendance of about twenty. The church is shared with a French Baptist congregation.

A stained-glass window

This scene includes a logger and is dedicated to Arthur Schmon, who managed McCormick's operation on the North Shore.

The McCormick dam
Shelter Bay (Port Cartier)

Before the coming of industrialists to this remote, little-known corner of Quebec, there were native hunters, some fishing and, of course, the fur trade. When the Clarke family and Col. McCormick arrived, there was only "...forest, bleak granite, and swift moving waters tumbling unchecked into the St. Lawrence". (A. Schmon)

In 1919, McCormick and his CEO at the Ontario Paper Co. Ltd. of Thorold, Ont., Arthur Schmon, began to develop operations at Shelter Bay. "We had to build, not only

dams, logging booms, wharves and water conveyers, but a townsite providing homes, schools, churches, power, water and other essential services." (A. Schmon) Isolation, loneliness and boredom were the lot of those stationed here, especially the wives of the workers. There was no travel by water between November and April. Mail came twice a month by dog sled.

This dam was built and a power house which brought electricity to the fledgling village. The dam was constructed near a holding basin for logs and the start of the flume. Shelter Bay became one of the first industrial communities on the North Shore.

The de-barking mill
Patterson Island, Shelter Bay (Port Cartier)

Tree bark was of no use to the paper companies. It had to be removed and burned before the logs were shipped. This is the Quebec North Shore Paper Co's first de-barking site. The interior structure is in the shape of a bowl where the bark was removed with large knives. The de-barked logs were then transported by the flume to the quay.

Patterson Island was named for Joseph Patterson, longtime president of Quebec North Shore.

The flume: a skeleton from the past
Shelter Bay (Port Cartier)

Before the development of major highways and flat-bed trucks, the logging industry depended upon the rivers and the flumes to transport logs to the St. Lawrence River.

This is the Quebec North Shore Co. flume, built in 1918. Logs were floated down the Rivière-aux-Rochers to a holding centre near the dam, de-barked at the mill, and sent on to the quay by flume. Pulpwood loading began here in 1921, whence it was shipped to Thorold, Ontario to be processed into paper.

Shelter Bay's first hospital

Quebec North Shore built this hospital in the 1920s as part of its inducement to bring businessmen and professionals to this isolated area. The hospital treated only male workers; women were treated at home. It closed in 1958 and this is now the Port Cartier City Hall.

The name of Shelter Bay was given to this community to encourage ships' captains to dock here. According to our guide Stan McGee, long-time resident and company employee, it was anything but a sheltered bay. The name has disappeared into the history books save for small reminders: a street named Shelter Bay, a few old buildings and the remains of McCormick's operation.

Port Cartier is mostly French-speaking, but some English-speakers remain. Riverview High School, said to have an enrolment which is fifty per cent English, is evidence of this.

With the help of native guides and French labour, English entrepreneurs and engineers pioneered what is now the modern city of Port Cartier. The Shelter Bay area is now Port Cartier Ouest.

The Quebec North Shore manager's house
Shelter Bay (Port Cartier)

This house was built circa 1920, in the early years of the development of Shelter Bay. The English managers of the company are said to have run a system feudal-like in its rigours. Workers needed the permission of the company to marry, to build a house, even to come out of the woods to attend church or to visit their families. Trucking was practiced, with workers beholden to the company store.

These stringencies led to the eventual failure of this company. When the Quebec – Port Cartier Mining Co. established here in the 1950s, many Quebec North Shore workers jumped ship to the new company.

This house is now a private residence over-looking the falls of the Rivière-aux-Rochers and the skeletons of Shelter Bay's past.

The Clarke Company hydro dam, *Ste. Marguerite River.*

Clarke City was the first industrial community on the North Shore. William Clarke, from Toronto, acquired the rights to the power of the Marguerite River from the Quebec government in 1901 for $15,000 and invested $200,000 himself. He built this dam and a mill nearby. In 1908, Clarke City had fifty families, stores, inns, a post office and a school. By the 1940s, it was the centre of North Shore development with a population of over two thousand.

The Clarke family, William and his sons, would become prominent on the North Shore, building, in addition to the power dam and paper mill, a short-track railroad and a town near where modern Seven Islands would emerge.

The Gulf Pulp & Paper locomotive
Clarke City (Seven Islands)

This Gulf Pulp & Paper Co. locomotive is a museum piece epitomizing the role of the Clarkes in the early 20th century on the North Shore. The pulp mill, which no longer

exists, stood nearby. Nine miles of track were laid between the mill and Seven Islands harbour. Pulp from the mill was transported to the Clarke quay, then shipped to the Ontario plant to be processed into paper for *The Chicago Tribune*. The company ceased operations in 1967.

"Le Château"
Clarke City (Seven Islands)

This was the summer home of Frank Clarke, son of William, who with his brother Desmond, founded the Clarke Steamship Co. These ships, forerunners of the *Nordik Express*, served the North Shore villages. The *Nordik Express* today plies the route between Rimouski, Anticosti and the Lower North Shore from Seven Islands to Blanc Sablon. Clarke ships also served the Magdalen Islands, Prince Edward Island, Murray Bay, Gaspé and Newfoundland.

Frank's family spent the school vacation here. He and another brother, Walter, came here regularly for business and fishing. Walter's house was destroyed by fire and in the 1940s this one became an "edifice à logements".

The Clarkes left a considerable legacy on the North Shore.

The Hudson's Bay Company fur post *Boul. des Montagnais, Seven Islands*

The magnificent harbour location of Seven Islands attracted fishermen, whalers and fur traders to this area for centuries. This is a replica of the Hudson's Bay Co. trading post, called the King's Post, which stood here from the mid-19th century. It was erected as a 1967 Centennial project.

Donald Smith worked for the Hudson's Bay Co. down-river at Mingan as a young man in the 1840s. He became Lord Strathcona and, in 1885, pounded in the Last Spike of the CPR.

The Catholic Church formed the oldest North Shore parish in the diocese here in the 17th century. A. P. Low, of the Canadian Geological Survey, discovered large deposits of iron ore here in the 1890s and Hollinger Consolidated and the M. A. Hanna Company acquired rights for exploration and development in the early 1940s. With the arrival of the Iron Ore Co. of Canada in the late 1940s, this sleepy village would become a thriving metropolis, now mostly French-speaking, with a considerable Montagnais population and some English.

Quebec North Shore and Labrador Railway cars from Labrador City
Iron Ore Co. of Canada operations, Seven Islands

The Moisie River which flows into the St. Lawrence at Seven Islands is famous for its salmon fishing. The American-owned Adams Club has welcomed American dignitaries since the 19th century. There were even iron works here in the 19th century.

But, it was the Iron Ore Co. of Canada, with iron mining operations at Schefferville and, later, at Labrador City, which began the modern Seven Islands. At the height of the Cold War, with the Berlin crisis of 1948 and the formation of NATO in 1949, corporations became intensely interested in iron production. In 1949, Iron Ore Co. of Canada was formed, incorporating Hollinger, Hanna and five American steel companies. Surveys for a railway to Schefferville were underway in 1951, the Quebec North Shore & Labrador Railway was built and, in 1954, the first shipment of iron ore was sent to Seven Islands.

This photo shows Quebec North Shore & Labrador Railway cars arriving with iron ore pellets and iron concentrate from Labrador City. From here, they are shipped around the world. The company, which employs 1,880 (500 at Seven Islands; the rest at Labrador City), processes sixteen million tons of iron ore per year. This company is one of the engines which run the city of Seven Islands.

An Iron Ore Co. manager's house
Rue Evangeline, Seven Islands

This spacious house, built by the company, was for the use of senior management. In the 1950s, all senior management were English; today, four managers are English-speakers and three are French.

Workers' houses
Rue Cartier, Seven Islands

These smaller houses were
built in the 1940s for company
workers, most of whom were
English. They were built close to
company operations. Most of the
occupants now speak French.

The original Protestant church
Rue Mgr. Blanche, Seven Islands

Built in the 1950s as a
Protestant church, this is now the
English Catholic church, called
Christ the King, which serves the
region. The current Protestant
church serves two congregations,
the Anglican (All Saints') and the
United.

The Flemming elementary school
Rue Brochu, Seven Islands

Here is an English school which is
educating predominantly English
students, now a rare occurrence in
remote or rural areas of Quebec. About
one thousand English still live in Seven
Islands. This elementary school, built in
the 1960s and named for an early
geologist, sends its students on to
another English school, Queen
Elizabeth High School, located nearby.

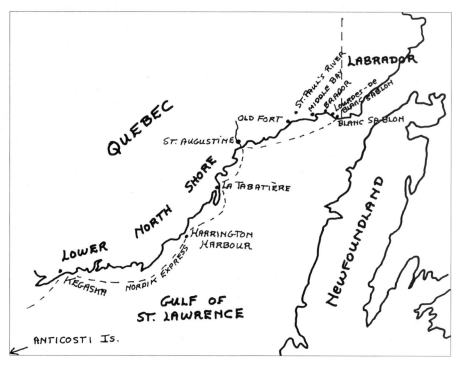

The Lower North Shore

The Lower North Shore begins at Kegaska and ends at Blanc Sablon near the Labrador border. The first European to sight this land was Jacques Cartier on his initial voyage in 1534. The bare hills of the Canadian Shield which reach these shores prompted Cartier to name it "the land God gave to Cain".

Three centuries later, in the 1830s, John James Audubon, the American ornithologist and painter of birds, both damned and praised this place as "a rocky desert...poor, miserable rugged country...not a square foot of soil," and "Wonderful! Wonderful! Wonderfully grand – aye, and terrific!"

The Lower North Shore attracted fishermen from Europe: Basque whalers, French sealers and cod-fishermen. Fishing stations were developed, but, for a long time, there were no permanent settlements. The sea's bounty drew them, not the soil. In the 19th century fisher-settlers began to arrive from Britain and the Channel Islands, from Acadia, Nova Scotia and Newfoundland.

The Coast, as the region is known locally, is comprised of sixteen villages: two Innu (La Romaine, which also has a French population, and Pakuashipi); one French (Tête-à-Baleine); one bilingual (Lourdes-de-Blanc-Sablon); and twelve with a majority English population. No road reaches this area from the heart of Quebec. Route 138 ends at Natashquan and from here the villages are accessible only by plane or boat. This is a sore subject for many in these communities.

The Coasters are a unique people. Hardy and independent, isolated, they are tremendously proud of their domain. Though they are geographically part of Quebec, in spirit they are more connected to Newfoundland. It is part of the ancestry of the majority and this is reflected in everything from speech patterns to architecture. Many feel that Quebec has forgotten them.

Our two-week journey to the Lower North Shore and Anticosti Island was truly memorable. We boarded the *Nordik Express* at Rimouski in the company of our son Patrick who is a photographer. This family voyage, by ship and by car, was blessed by good fortune and was one of the real highlights of our travels throughout Quebec.

Charlie McCormick's house

Port Menier (Anticosti)

Our good fortune began on our first day at sea. We were scheduled for a two-hour stop at Port Menier. We knew that the English settlement at Anticosti had been on the opposite side of this large island, an impossibility for us to visit, and we had not been able to confirm any landmarks in Port Menier. The significant historic name that our research had turned up was that of Charlie McCormick.

One of our fellow passengers was wearing a shirt emblazoned *Anticosti*. He turned out to be Danny McCormick, a francophone, grandson of Charlie, and he was offering a tour of the Port Menier area during our stopover. This was the first of many serendipitous occurrences on this trip.

Port Menier was named for French chocolate millionaire Henri Menier who bought Anticosti for $125,000 in 1895. He proceeded like a seigneur. All on the island were to abide by "Menier's Law". The small contingent of English settlers at Fox Bay on the eastern shore of the island were told to walk to Port Menier, or to leave. Most took the latter option, many emigrating to the Lower North Shore. Menier developed the village, building houses and a school and a grand chateau for himself which burned to the ground in 1954. In 1926, the Menier family sold the island to Consolidated-Bathurst Co. which promoted lumbering for pulpwood.

Charlie McCormick, a lad of nineteen, arrived at this time to work as a lumberjack. His grandfather Michael McCormick had emigrated from Ireland and subsequently worked in the forests of the Ottawa Valley for the MacKenzie Brothers Company. Charlie enjoyed the pastimes of salmon-fishing and deer-hunting and gained a reputation as an expert in both. When Consolidated-Bathurst stopped cutting in 1972 due to the costs of both forest fires and transportation, Charlie McCormick convinced the Quebec government to make the island a fishing and hunting preserve. He was named supervisor of the island which he would turn into a sportsmen's paradise.

Lumberjack, guide, overseer of forest operations and of sports hunting and fishing, responsible for protecting fauna, superintendent of the village and justice of the peace, "the boss", "monsieur Charlie", wore many hats and left a legacy for Anticosti which remains to this day: preservation of the flora and fauna and creation of a tourist industry which has attracted such luminaries as Rockefellers, Desmarais and Trudeaus. A lake on the island is named Lake Charlie.

This house, built by Menier in 1901, was Charlie's home for many years. In the 1940s, he moved to a small modern bungalow where his grandson Danny lives today.

The Charlie McCormick headstone
The Catholic cemetery, Port Menier

Here lies Charlie McCormick and his family reads the inscription on this headstone.

Charlie, an Irish Catholic, married Florence Noel, an Anticostienne; their descendants are part of the French community.

On the morning of the day he died in 1982, according to his grandson Danny, Charlie landed a fourteen-pound salmon on his beloved Jupiter River. Charlie McCormick is fondly remembered in this community.

Crab boats
Kegaska

Kegaska, or "Kaska" as it is known here, is the first community at the western end of the Coast. There is archaeological evidence that the Montagnais camped here in summer. The Hudson's Bay Co. founded a salmon-fishing and trading post here as early as 1831; and in the 1850s, several Acadian families arrived from the Magdalen Islands, but either disease or economic conditions, or perhaps both, drove them away in the early 1870s.

The English who populate the village today are descendants of settlers who came from Newfoundland, Labrador, Anticosti, Great Britain and the Channel Islands from the mid to the late 19th century. Once a thriving fishing village, Kegaska has seen its fish plant close except as a holding facility for the Daley Bros. fish processing plant at La Tabatière. The harbour is still used by local fishermen. Crab-fishing has replaced cod-fishing since the early 1990s.

Foreman's sawmill
Kegaska

Our contact in Kegaska was Leslie Foreman, a retired sawmill operator now in his 80s. We had hoped to contact him by cell phone from the *Nordik Express*, but found that our cell would not work in this area. So, we would dock, phone him, and hope for the best. The stop here was a short one. As we disembarked, we saw a man, clearly local, greeting other arrivals. "Could you tell us where we'd find Leslie Foreman?" we asked him. "That's me," he replied and we knew our luck was holding.

Leslie Foreman ran this sawmill for over fifty years, closing it in 1997. When in operation, the mill had piles of wood and logs outside which stretched the length of two city blocks. Most of the houses in Kegaska were built with wood sawed at Foreman's mill. "All but the four newest," he said. The saw was run by an engine which he salvaged from a lighthouse at Cape Riddle.

Samuel Foreman, great-grandfather of Leslie, arrived in Kegaska in the 1850s from Nova Scotia to fish for salmon. He was seventy years old at the time. The Foremans would be joined by English-speaking refugees forced out of Menier's Anticosti and others from Ontario. Many of their descendants live in Kegaska today. The Quebec government, recognizing the role that the Foremans played here over the last one hundred and fifty years, sent Leslie a form to fill out which would allow them to rename the local Salmon River, the Foreman River. Leslie, who cannot read French, didn't reply.

So, it is still the Salmon River.

St. Philip's Church
Kegaska

St. Philip's Anglican Church took four years to build in the 1950s and was opened in 1959. Leslie Foreman cut 15,000 feet of board for the task for which the church paid him twenty dollars. Most early churches were built mainly by volunteer labour, but we thought that this seemed a bit much. Wouldn't happen today, Leslie assured us. "My dear woman, today, nobody works for nothing."

The Kegaska cemetery
Local volunteer labour cleared the trees from this tract of land to create an English

cemetery. Quebecois road workers from Natashquan pulled out the stumps without charge. "They wouldn't take a cent. Not even a tank of fuel," Leslie Foreman told us. Names on the headstones here include: Mansbridge, Strickland and Kippen.

The Robertson seal foundry
Spar Point, La Tabatière

La Tabatière was the centre of the seal hunt on the Coast as far back as the hunting and fishing concessions during the French régime. When the Labrador Company, which had a post here, went bankrupt in the 1820s, former employee Samuel John Robertson, an Orkneyman, purchased the post. He settled at Spar Point in the harbour of La Tabatière and is considered the founder of the village. Robertson received John James Audubon here in the 1830s.

Robertson's descendants still live here. Shown, is his great-great-grandson Russell Robertson. Aged eighty-three (2002), he started to work at fourteen. Three years in a fish plant were followed by his career with the post office: captain of the mail boat in season, delivering mail by dog-sled in winter to as far away as St. Augustine.

From the height of Spar Point, Russell Robertson showed us where the seals swam into the harbour to be trapped by the seal-hunters. After the slaughter, the blubber was hauled up to this seal foundry, one of the last remaining in Quebec. The process involved cutting up the blubber in the box (left of photo), throwing it into the vat (centre) and boiling it; the scrunch (oil) was then released into drums (on the right) for transport. This operation was run for generations by the Robertson family. Russell is proud of this old foundry and wants to preserve it as a part of Coast history. Others call it an eyesore and want it demolished. So far, history is winning.

The split house *Spar Point, La Tabatière*

Before the development of fish plants, fish processing took place in the split house and the stage. Cornelius Walsh of Blanc Sablon described the process to us: the split house stood on a wharf next to the water; fish were unloaded into a large box; placed on the splitting table where the throat was cut and the belly sliced open; guts and liver removed; head broken; the fish was de-boned; cleaned in a tub of water; and brought to the stage for salting and storing, ready for transport.

Split houses are hard to find nowadays. Small, messy and smelly, they have not inspired people to save them and use them for other purposes.

St. Andrew's Church
La Tabatière

La Tabatière comes from the Montagnais word for sorcerer, Tabquen. The Montagnais consulted the sorcerer for omens before their hunting trips inland.

Today, La Tabatière (pronounced locally, Tabatcher) is a grouping of three fishing hamlets: La Tabatière, Red Bay and Old Post. The settlers here came from England, France, the Channel Islands and Newfoundland. Most, today, are English-speaking.

This Anglican church was built mostly (including the pews) by carpenter Loyal Mansbridge of Mutton Bay, whom we met on the *Nordik Express*. He was moving back home after relocating with his wife to Seven Islands to be close to a large hospital. They missed Mutton Bay and, given the waiting time for hospital appointments, decided that the air transport to St. Anthony's Hospital in Newfoundland or to Seven Islands was worth the risk.

This church, only thirty years old (most buildings on the coast are relatively new), is lucky to get a service once a month when a minister comes from Harrington Harbour.

The wharf at La Tabatière

In 1952, the Louis Blais factory for rendering seal oil, which was no longer profitable, closed. The building was transformed into a fish-processing plant, the largest on the Coast, for crab and scallops. Today, Daley Bros. from Newfoundland owns the plant and is the principal employer of the region.

Here, we see crab being off-loaded from the *Baffin Fjord*. Pictured is a young Fequet (a well-known name here; once French – Féquet – it is now pronounced Feckey).

The wharf was very lively during our stopover. The *Nordik Express,* which is a supply ship for these outposts, unloaded her cargo and local passengers. The workers on the boats and on the wharf are all men; those in the processing plant are eighty per cent women, many of whom have held their jobs for over twenty years.

"The Rambler"
La Tabatière

Fishing boats like *The Rambler* are still made by local fishermen who had to learn to make their own boats. The hull is sided with local spruce wood and the inside supports are made of juniper. A boat should last ten to twelve years, we were told, fourteen if well-cared for.

Harrington Harbour village

This little gem of a village sits on an island, accessible only by boat or helicopter. It is built on rock which forms part of the landscape. A tracery of boardwalks crisscrosses the rock, linking the houses and acting as both sidewalk for pedestrians and roadway for the four-wheelers and bicycles. There are no cars. Colourful wooden houses, some on stilts, abound. The population is about two hundred and eighty-five.

John Chislet and Benjamin Simms came here from Fortune Bay, Newfoundland, in the later 19th century, seeking fish and a good harbour. The first log cabin was built in 1871 and other settlers began to arrive. It is still a lively harbour, with fishing boats and a crab-processing plant. A popular Quebec film, *La Grande Séduction* (2003), was shot here with this town standing in for the fictional Ste-Marie-la-Mauderne.

Christ Church
Harrington Harbour

This church, originally Anglican, now serves both Anglican and United congregations. The first church was built in 1898; this one in 1953. A boardwalk leads to the church whose walls display memorials to those lost at sea.

The Grenfell mission
Harrington Harbour

Wilfred Grenfell, English doctor and pastor, founded a mission hospital here in 1907. It was the only hospital on the Lower North Shore at the time and Harrington Harbour became known as "hospital island".

Dr. Donald Gordon Hodd joined the mission, of which he later became head, in 1926. Until 1970, the Grenfell mission provided medical services to the Coast, from Natashquan to Labrador. Dr. Hodd, who in the early years, served some of the communities by dog-sled, was awarded the Order of Canada in 1976.

The building has since been modernized and made into a residence for seniors – the Hodd Residence. Dave King of Kegaska, whom we met on the *Nordik Express*, extolled the quality of care given here.

"The Puffin" , *St. Augustine wharf.*

The boat ride up the St. Augustine river is spectacular: rock walls and inlets, waves breaking on the shore, the spare vegetation found all along the Coast. The ship docks at a wharf six kilometers from the town of St. Augustine.

This was a fishing and sealing post during the French and early British eras. French- and English-speakers from Quebec and Newfoundland settled here in the later 19th century. Today, it is one of the largest villages on the Coast with a population of nine hundred and thirty, mainly English-speaking.

Shown here is Clayton Pilgrim, from Newfoundland, twenty-seven-year resident of St. Augustine, former bush pilot and engaging conversationalist. "Trying to make a silk purse out of this sow's ear," he said of his efforts to transform *The Puffin*, once a crab-fishing boat, into a cabin cruiser. His retirement dream is to take small groups out to fish the nearby waters. He considers the Coast to be a "part of Newfoundland".

The Walsh stage
Blanc Sablon

Blanc Sablon, situated near the Strait of Belle Isle which separates Labrador and Newfoundland, has a long maritime history. Basque whalers came here in the 16th century, followed by cod-fishers and seal-hunters from Spain, Portugal and France (Jacques Cartier mentions Blanc Sablon). Jersey Islanders came to fish in the 18th century, Canadiens in the 19th century and Newfoundlanders, brought over by the Job Bros. Co, in the late 19th century.

Today, Blanc Sablon remains a fishing village; it has a deep-water port which can accommodate longliners and trawlers, a fish plant and a ferry which transports passengers and goods between Quebec and St. Barbe, Newfoundland. The population is mainly English-speaking.

Here we see Cornelius Walsh, holding an old cod net, standing next to the stage built by his grandfather Luke Patrick Walsh in the 1920s. When Patrick Walsh arrived in Blanc Sablon from Nameless Cove, Newfoundland, he found that the entire shoreline had been claimed by other fishermen. So, he built his stage on stilts on the off-shore rocks (background in photo). Later, he built this stage at the high-water mark – legally, public land. He married a Coast girl.

The stage was the hut where a fisherman salted his catch and placed it in layers ready for transportation. He had to do this carefully because compression could result in loss of weight. Cornelius has created a summer camp here where he can get away from the mosquitos and black flies. He says that some people feel seasick when the tide comes in underneath.

Cornelius now runs a restaurant to which he gave his own childhood nickname – *Sputnik*. The Office de la Langue Française forced him to change this to *Spoutnik*. Cornelius is not amused. "It's a Russian name!" he points out.

The Hudson's Bay Company store
Blanc Sablon

Hudson's Bay stores supplied goods ranging from food and clothing to outboard motors to the isolated villages of the Lower North Shore. General stores were few in number, so the Hudson's Bay Co. was a lifeline until the later 20th century. Then, they were gradually phased out as other stores opened up. Some of the premises were bought by local businessmen. This store closed in the late 1980s.

The Lourdes/Blanc Sablon cemetery
Route 138 between Lourdes-de-Blanc-Sablon and Blanc Sablon.

English and French Catholics are buried side-by-side in this cemetery, with the hills of Labrador in the distance: French Catholics from Lourdes-de-Blanc-Sablon and English Catholics from Blanc Sablon and Middle Bay with names such as Jones, Walsh and Buckle. In June, the cemeteries of the Coast are filled with bouquets and wreaths.

The Petit Havre fish plant
Lourdes-de-Blanc-Sablon

One of the larger villages on the Coast, with a population of 750 in 1997, Lourdes-de-Blanc-Sablon has both a French and an English history.

Fishermen from Jersey and Newfoundland fished from here and, circa 1824, Charles Dicker from Newfoundland settled here. The English call it Long Point; it is on a rocky point where three of Captain James Cook's benchmarks (the highwater mark) have been located by local historians.

French-speakers from the St. Lawrence valley and the Gaspé arrived in the mid-19th century and became the majority. The Catholic Church retained it as a French community despite inter-marriage with those from Jersey and Newfoundland. Their descendants live here today; although the majority are French, most are bilingual. In 1907, the village was re-named Lourdes-de-Blanc-Sablon in honour of Notre Dame de Lourdes, in France.

It was on Greenly Island, three kilometers off-shore from the village, that the German Junkers monoplane *Bremen* landed in 1928. En route from Ireland to North America, on the first east-to-west trans-Atlantic flight, one year after Lindbergh's historic solo, the *Bremen* was forced to land here due to violent weather and low fuel.

The Petit Havre fish plant was a community enterprise (co-op). It has been closed since the late 1990s, a fate which has befallen many Coast fish plants.

Saint Christopher's Church
Brador

Saint Christopher's, an Anglican church built in 1969, stands on the Brador Plain surrounded by the stark hills and water falls of the Canadian Shield. About one hundred and fifty people live here now. Their story is a familiar one on the Coast. This area has been used as a base of operations by Basque whalers, French cod-fishermen (at one time, up to 150 cod-fishing boats made port here in summer), Jersey fishermen and British seal-hunters and fishermen. Permanent settlement, mostly Newfoundlanders, finally came in the late 19th century. Their descendants remain today: Etheridges, Harts, Hobbses.

Puffin Island (Île des Perroquets) is one of the offshore bird sanctuaries on this part of the Coast. It has the largest puffin colony in Quebec. A local fisherman agreed to take us out – to land, we expected; but, since this is a bird sanctuary, that is forbidden. So, he circled the island, in very choppy waters, while we bounced (ouch!), and photographed, and bounced (ouch!), and looked through our binoculars at the murres and puffins which wheeled about us and clustered on the rocks. The puffin, symbol of the Coast, tropical in appearance, is a hardy little bird which winters in the northern waters off Newfoundland. Puffin Island is one of its nesting grounds.

Brador Coastline

The general store
Middle Bay

Harold Lavallee (here pronounced La Valley) remembers catching cod as a boy and eating it in a shack near the fish plant after a day's fishing with his father, a cod and crab fisherman. Harold's grandfather was French; his maternal grandmother was Irish – a Buckle, a well-known Coaster name. Lavallee is today the most common name in Middle Bay; they are English-speaking.

This is a true general store. It offers goods ranging from food to wool, from tools to books, and services such as a Post Office and butchering facilities. In 2002, Harold won a government award for his forty years operating this general store.

The children of Middle Bay – with a population of one hundred, one of the smallest of the Lower North Shore villages – go to a primary school in St. Paul's River, the next village. Many leave the Coast for further education, some going to Alexander Galt High School in Lennoxville. Both of Harold's children have left the Coast, a story repeated many times over in this part of the province.

Stages and Smith's fish plant
Middle Bay

Middle Bay was settled by French Quebecers and English Newfoundlanders in the later 19th century. Remains of a Basque whaling station have been found here indicating that it was used as a port long before settlement arrived. The main language today is English, though many people have French names.

Lined up along the wharf near to the fish plant stand the old stages, once so important to the fishermen. Smith's, a co-op fish plant, processed cod and lump fish. Today, with the end of the cod fishery, it is only in partial use. To the right of the fish plant in the photo stands the stage which belonged to Harold Lavallee's father. In the white shack behind, young Harold and his friends once ate the cod they had caught that day.

"Miss Brodie's Hill"
St. Paul's River

Jane Brodie, a Montrealer of Scottish descent, worked as a missionary-teacher for the Canada Foreign Missionary Society. She began her work in 1860 on nearby Caribou Island where Congregationalists had set up the first permanent mission on the Lower North Shore. For many years, Jane Brodie lived in a house at the bottom of this hill which stands behind the village where she died in 1906 at the age of eighty-seven. She is buried in Mount Royal cemetery in Montreal, but her memory lives on in St. Paul's River with this hill named in her honour.

"Dwight's" cemetery
Old Fort Bay

Dwight Bilodeau is a veritable fixture in old Fort Bay. In addition to running the general store, Dwight donates a great deal of his time to improving the quality of life of

this community of three hundred and fifty and to preserving its heritage. He is English-speaking, as are all in Old Fort Bay, though many like him have French surnames.

One of his many projects is the renewal and care of this cemetery, affectionately known as "Dwight's" cemetery, next to St. Peter's Church. For the past fifteen years Dwight has been reclaiming headstones once covered with sand. "These graves deserve a marking,' he says, "since they are our past. These are the people who settled our

250

community and helped make it what it is today." He now has the names of ninety people buried here, eighty percent of whom have no markings. Names on the headstones include those of Fequet, Bilodeau and Buckle.

This stone commemorates Beatrice Buckle (1913-1931) who drowned just before her marriage and was buried in her wedding dress. Legend has it that a water dog which wanted to go to her was held back by a girl who had her eye on Beatrice's fiancé.

Fishing boats
Old Fort Bay

A local resident, excavating his basement, came upon what is believed to be the remains of Le Vieux Fort constructed by the French in the 1700s. The protection of the

bay made this an ideal site for fishing. After the Conquest, fishermen from Gaspé (Robin, Féquet) and Newfoundland (Buckle, Hayward) settled here.

Route 138 gives access to Natashquan and from there ferries take passengers and goods down river and to Newfoundland. However, access to Lower North Shore villages can only be made by boat, plane or ski-doo since the main highway down the North Shore, route 138, ends just beyond Natashquan, isolating the Coasters from the rest of Quebec. Dwight Bilodeau says, "We feel closer to Newfoundland than anything in Quebec. Newfoundland is our province." He, like many others, has mixed feelings about the proposed extension of route 138 to Kegaska and on to Old Fort Bay.

Coasters love their unique village culture and their freedom, but the population is shrinking. Young workers leave home in the summer for seasonal jobs in other parts of Quebec and Canada and, though some return home in the winter, some do not. Many of those who leave for secondary and higher education remain away to find jobs. Returning for holidays and family events is difficult because of the high cost of transportation. For many, it is an agonizing trade-off: isolation, freedom, culture versus better communication, economic development, jobs, population stability, family reunions, etc. And, as Dwight put it, "People would have to lock their doors."

These boats, *Gallant Traveller, Trudy Rhonda* and *Becky Lee Robin* (boat names consisting of two or three girls' names usually honour the daughters of the fisherman) still fish out of Old Fort Bay. However, the fish plant is closed and the *Nordik Express* no longer calls here. How long will the crab and scallop fishery last? Would a through road eventually change the English nature of these villages? These are big questions which await their answer.

Fish plant at Old Fort Bay

Marvin Buckle, seen here repairing his twelve-year old fishing boat, was formerly the manager of the Old Fort Bay fish plant. The government is in the process of buying back fishing licenses, so an ever fewer number make their living from the sea. The cod fishery has closed; there is no longer a commercial salmon fishery. The raison d'être for the appearance of these villages in the 19th century is slowly disappearing. Ninety-five per cent of the working-age population who winter here live on Employment Insurance.

John Crosbie, former federal fisheries minister who led the move to end the cod fishery in 1992, warned in 2002 of a similar fate for Newfoundland's lucrative shellfish (crab and shrimp) industry. Is the government licensing too many shellfish plants as they once licensed too many cod plants?

In 2003, Fisheries and Oceans Canada ended snow crab fishing in the easterly part of the Lower North Shore. Danny Dumaresque, president of Blanc Sablon Sea Foods, focuses on other catches such as scallops, whelk, Stimson clams, sea urchins and lump fish roe "the poor man's caviar". Since fishing has always been the mainstay of the Lower North Shore villages, Dumaresque believes that the governments should help the cod and crab fishermen to diversify their catches by assisting in the purchase of new equipment and the finding of new markets. "The world is out there, ready to take all our species," he says. This is the least that governments can do for a people whose whole history has revolved around the sea.

Wood piles, Lower North Shore style

The distinctive, teepee-shape of these wood piles, similar to those found in Newfoundland, symbolizes the historic cultural connection of the Lower North Shore with that province.

Selected Bibliography

Abbott, L. A Country So Wild and Grand. St. Paul's River: Coasters Association Inc., 1999.

Abbott, L. The Coast Way. Montreal: McGill-Queen's University Press, 1988.

Annet, K. Gaspé of Yesterday. (many volumes of articles, beginning in 1980).

Atlas Historique du Québec. Québec, Ville et Capitale. Ste-Foy: La Presse de l'Université Laval, 2001.

Baldwin, A. Metis, wee Scotland of the Gaspé. Canada: A.S.Baldwin, 1960. (1977 printing)

Baldwin, A. The Price Family, Pioneers of the Saguenay. Canada: A.S.Baldwin, 1978.

Beattie, B. Tadoussac: The Sands of Summer. Montreal: Price-Patterson, 1994.

Bernier, A. Le Vieux-Sillery. Québec: Gouvernement du Québec, 1982.

Blair, L. "Tu te Souviens" (The Literary and Historical Society of Quebec). The Canadian   Forum. May, 1998.

Boissonault, R. Les Forges du Saint-Maurice, 1729-1883. Ottawa: Minister of Supplies and Services Canada, 1983.

Breakey, A. "Breakey, John", Dictionary of Canadian Biography, vol.XIV, pp.139-140. Toronto: University of Toronto
        Press.

Brotherton, G. et al. Pabos, Site Historique et Archéologique. Société Historique de la Gaspésie, 1985.

Cabot, F. The Greater Perfection. The Story of the Gardens at Les Quatre Vents. N.Y.: W.W.Norton and Company,
        2001.

Campbell, D. Global Mission, The Story of Alcan. vol.I. Ontario Publishing Co. Ltd., 1985.

Caron, F. Fred C. Wurtele Photographe. Québec: Ministières des Affaires Culturelles, 1977.

Cascapedia Bay Heritage: a History of New Richmond and Environs. New Richmond Heritage Group, 1980.

Census (of Lower Canada), 1860-61.

Charbonneau, A. et al. Quebec the Fortified City: From the 17th Century to the 19th Century. Ottawa: Parks
        Canada, 1982.

Clark, B. Gleanings on the Magdalen Islands. Council for Anglophone Magdalen Islanders, 2000.

Deveau, L. et al. Where Green is Worn – Shannon. Montmagny: Editions Marquis Ltée., 1983.

Dickinson, J. and Young, B. A Short History of Quebec. (second edition) Montreal: McGill-Queen's University Press,
        2000.

Dionne, L. and Pelletier, G. Cacouna, les Randonnées du Passé. Quebec: Minister of Culture and Communications,
        1995.

Dubé, P. Deux Cents Ans de Villégiature dans Charlevoix. Québec: Les Presses de l'Université Laval, 1986.

Duguay, A. Rivière-du-Loup: At the Heart of Its Memories. Quebec: Ministry of Culture and Communications, 1997.

Evans, L. Tides of Tadoussac. Montreal: Price-Patterson, 1982.

Francis, R. et al. Destinies: Canadian History Since Confederation. Toronto: H.R.&W., 1988.

Gauthier, L. Centenaire de Portneuf, 1861-1961. (translation by T.B.B.Ford) 1961.

Geren, R. and McCulloch, B. Cain's Legacy, the Building of Iron Ore Company of Canada. Sept Îles: I.O.C., 1990.

Greening, W.E. "Trois-Rivières, Historic Gateway to the Saint-Maurice", Canadian Geographical Journal. Ottawa:
        May, 1981.

Guay, M.. The Fortifications of Quebec. Quebec and Ottawa: Parks Canada, 1998.

Heritage Trails. Old Quebec City. (brochure) Quebec Anglophone Heritage Network.

"History of the Parish of Donnacona". Quebec Telegraph, November 4, 1916.

Jeffrey Hale's Hospital Centre, 1865-1990, 1990.

Lambert, S. and Roy, C. Une Histoire d'Appartenance. La Côte-Nord. Ste-Foy: Les Éditions GID, 2001.

Lanken, D. "Summers Down the St. Lawrence", Canadian Geographic, April-May, 1987.

Manning, H.T. The Revolt of French Canada, 1800-1835. Toronto: Macmillan, 1962.

McCormick, C. Anticosti. St.-Nazaire-de-Chicoutimi: Les Éditions JCL Inc., 1979.

McDougall, D. "The Gaspé Loyalists", <u>Loyalist Gazette</u>, vol.XXI, no.2. Concordia University.

O'Gallagher, M. <u>Grosse Île, Gateway to Canada, 1832-1937</u>. Ste-Foy: Carraig Books, 1984.

O'Gallagher, M. <u>Saint Patrick's, Quebec</u>. Quebec: Carraig Books, 1981.

O'Gallagher, M. <u>The Shamrock Trail. Tracing the Irish in Quebec City</u>. Ste-Foy: Carraig Books.

<u>Old Manors Old Houses</u>. Quebec: Historic Monuments Commission of the Province of Quebec, 1927.

<u>Parish Record – Saint Stephen's Church, Grand'mere, P.Q.</u> (1880-1923).

Poulin, A-M. <u>Christ Church in Frampton</u>. Bibliothèque Nationale du Québec, 1989.

Reisner, M. <u>Strangers and Pilgrims</u>. A History of the Anglican Diocese of Quebec, 1793-1993. Toronto: Anglican Book Centre, 1995.

Richardson, A. <u>et al</u>. <u>Quebec City: Architects, Artisans and Builders</u>. Ottawa: National Museum of Man, 1984.

Rouillard, E. <u>La Côte Nord du Saint-Laurent et le Labrador Canadien</u>. Québec: Laflamme et Proulx, 1908.

Roxborough, H. <u>One Hundred – Not Out. The Story of Nineteenth Century Canadian Sport</u>. Toronto: Ryerson Press, 1966.

Ruddell, D. <u>Québec City: 1765-1832</u>. Ottawa: Canadian Museum of Civilization, 1987.

Rudin, R. <u>The Forgotten Quebecers</u>. Quebec: Institut Québecois de Recherche sur la Culture, 1985.

Sack, B. <u>History of the Jews in Canada</u>. Montreal: Harvest House, 1965.

Saywell, J. <u>The Canadian Journal of Lady Aberdeen, 1893-1898</u>. Toronto: The Champlain Society, 1960.

<u>Shawinigan Water and Power Company</u>. 1932.

Solway, D. "Moments in Murray Bay", <u>Town and Country</u>. August, 1988.

Smith, H. <u>Shelter Bay</u>. Montreal: McClelland and Stewart, 1964.

Treggett, B. and Bergeron, S. <u>Mount Hermon Cemetery</u>. 1988.

Vézina, R. <u>Holidays in Old Quebec</u>. Quebec:The Board of Trade of the District of Québec, 1966.

<u>Vieux Québec, Son Architecture Intérieure</u>.

Wallace, W. <u>The Macmillan Dictionary of Canadian Biography</u>. Toronto: Macmillan, 1963.

Willson, B. <u>Quebec, the Laurentian Province</u>. London: Constable Co., 1913.

<u>Newspapers</u>

The Gazette (Montreal).

The Quebec Chronicle-Telegraph (Quebec City).

The Quebec Heritage News (Q.A.H.N.)

SPEC (New Carlisle).

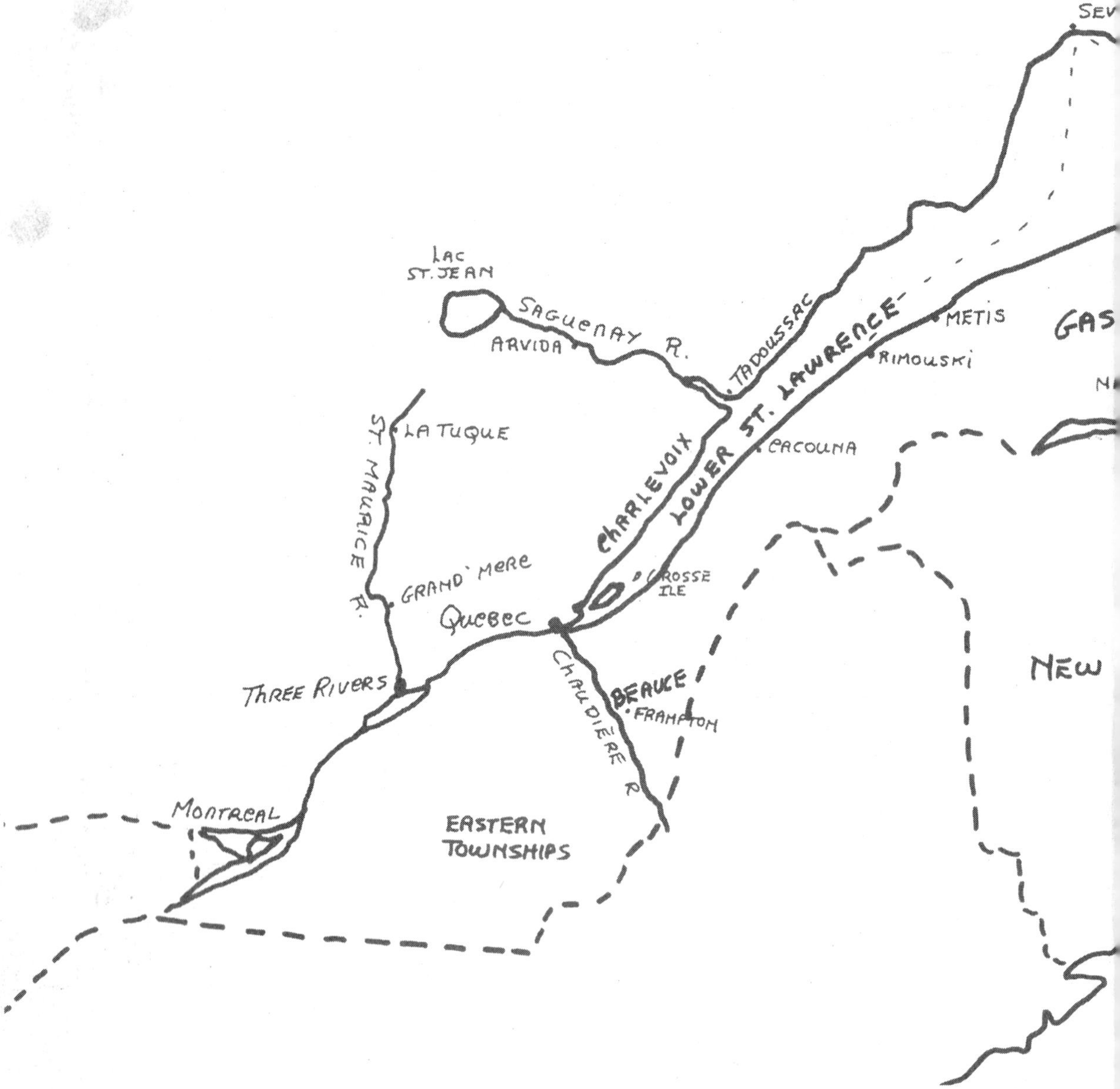

LAC ST. JEAN
SAGUENAY R.
ARVIDA
TADOUSSAC
LOWER ST. LAWRENCE
METIS
RIMOUSKI
CACOUNA
CHARLEVOIX
ST. MAURICE R.
LA TUQUE
GRAND' MERE
GROSSE ILE
QUEBEC
THREE RIVERS
BEAUCE
FRAMPTON
CHAUDIÈRE R.
MONTREAL
EASTERN TOWNSHIPS
NEW